Advance Praise for *Customer Mania!*

"In the long history of management writing, no one has so clearly and memorably extracted, exposed, illustrated, and explained the essentials of enlightened and profitable management as Ken Blanchard. Now he, with Jim Ballard and Fred Finch, offers us the ultimate customer service book, *Customer Mania!* The title is a dead giveaway of the passionate and persuasive argument contained in these pages. Bravo!"

—TOM PETERS

"If you depend on satisfied customers to keep your bottom line strong, you just got a gift in this book."
—HARVEY MACKAY, author of *Swim with the Sharks Without Being Eaten Alive*

"*Customer Mania!* offers an extraordinary example of roll up your sleeves, get in the trenches, know the details, build the team, and take the mountain. Ken Blanchard and his coauthors have found the perfect model in the Yum! organization."
—JAMIE DIMON, president and chief operating officer, JP Morgan Chase

"If you've hoped for wisdom that gives you a clear template for building outstandingly successful customer service, *Customer Mania!* provides a superb road map with clear driving instructions. P&Ls only tell you where you've been, not where you're going. If you do the right things, and this book tells you what they are, the P&Ls will take care of themselves."
—JEANETTE SARKISIAN WAGNER, vice chairman emerita, The Estée Lauder Companies Inc.

*f*P

The Secret: What Great Leaders Know—And Do *(with Mark Miller)*, *2004*

The Leadership Pill™ *(with Marc Muchnick)*, *2003*

Full Steam Ahead! *(with Jesse Stoner)*, *2003*

The One Minute Apology: A Powerful Way to Make Things Better *(with Margret McBride)*, *2003*

Whale Done!®: The Power of Positive Relationships *(with Thad Lacinak, Chuck Tompkins, and Jim Ballard)*, *2002*

High Five! *(with Sheldon Bowles)*, *2001*

Management of Organizational Behavior: Utilizing Human Resources *(with Paul Hersey)*, *8th edition, 2000*

Leadership by the Book *(with Bill Hybels and Phil Hodges)*, *1999*

The Heart of a Leader, *1999*

Gung Ho!® *(with Sheldon Bowles)*, *1998*

Raving Fans®: A Revolutionary Approach to Customer Service *(with Sheldon Bowles)*, *1993*

Managing by Values *(with Michael O'Connor)*, *1997*

Mission Possible *(with Terry Waghorn)*, *1996*

Empowerment Takes More Than a Minute *(with John P. Carlos and Alan Randolph)*, *1996*

Everyone's a Coach *(with Don Shula)*, *1995*

We Are the Beloved, *1994*

The One Minute Manager Builds High Performing Teams *(with Don Carew and Eunice Parisi-Carew)*, *1990*

The Power of Ethical Management *(with Norman Vincent Peale)*, *1988*

Leadership and the One Minute Manager *(with Patricia Zigarmi and Drea Zigarmi)*, *1985*

Putting the One Minute Manager to Work *(with Robert Lorber)*, *1984*

The One Minute Manager® *(with Spencer Johnson)*, *1982*

Managing for Organizational Effectiveness *(with Halsey Jones and Joseph Litterer)*, *1976*

What's the Rush?, *1999*

Mind Like Water, *2004*

Customer
MANIA!

It's NEVER Too Late to Build a Customer-Focused Company

KEN BLANCHARD

JIM BALLARD

FRED FINCH

FREE PRESS

NEW YORK   LONDON   TORONTO   SYDNEY

$f\!P$

FREE PRESS
A Division of Simon & Schuster, Inc.
1230 Avenue of the Americas
New York, NY 10020

For information about special discounts for bulk purchases,
please contact Simon & Schuster Special Sales:
1-800-456-6798 or business@simonandschuster.com

Designed by Lisa Chovnick

Manufactured in the United States of America

1   3   5   7   9   10   8   6   4   2

LLibrary of Congress Cataloging-in-Publication Data
Blanchard, Kenneth H.
Customer mania!: it's never too late to build a customer-focused company /
Ken Blanchard, Jim Ballard, Fred Finch.
p.   cm.
1. Customer services—Management.   I. Ballard, Jim, 1933–.
II. Finch, Frederic E.   III. Title.
HF5415.5 .B256   2004
658.8'12—dc22   2004056398

ISBN 0-7432-7028-2

THIS BOOK

IS DEDICATED TO ALL

THE LEADERS IN THE WORLD WHO ARE COMMITTED

TO MAKING A POSITIVE DIFFERENCE IN

THE LIVES OF THEIR PEOPLE AND THE

CUSTOMERS THEY SERVE.

CONTENTS

PART I

The Do-Over

CHAPTER 1

Yum! Meets the One Minute Manager

I HAVE THE GREATEST job in the world. I travel hither and yon, observing how organizations behave. I'm always looking for companies that are trying to build themselves the right way—by focusing on their customers and creating people-first, performance-based cultures.

Why is customer focus so important? Because whether you're selling pizzas or professional services, your business is not about you. It's about the people you serve. I say I'm always looking for companies that are trying to do it right because building a company the right way is a continuous journey. There is no final destination. When I find an organization on this journey, I am excited.

THE BEGINNING

Four years ago I was asked to speak about customer service to an annual meeting of KFC (originally Kentucky Fried Chicken). At that conference I met David Novak, who at the time was president of Tricon—the parent company of KFC, Taco Bell, and Pizza Hut. During that meeting, David told me about the journey he and his folks were on to revitalize a lackluster balance sheet by becoming a customer-centric organization. David knew that his company, like most companies, had already been giving lip service to focusing on the customer. He believed that building a company the right way meant going beyond merely listening and responding to the customer; it meant putting together a can-do team that was obsessed to go the

3

extra mile for the customer. David intended to create nothing short of a Customer Mania culture throughout all their restaurants worldwide.

Talk about an ambitious dream. In 1997 KFC, Taco Bell, and Pizza Hut had been spun off from PepsiCo to form Tricon. At that time, Tricon's balance sheet was in trouble. The new company had inherited a $4.7 billion debt and its return on invested capital hovered at a feeble 8 to 9 percent. As if that weren't a big enough challenge, in 2002 Tricon bought two additional quick service restaurant brands—Long John Silver's and A&W All American Food Restaurants—and in the process became by far the largest restaurant company in the world, employing some 840,000 people at nearly 33,000 restaurants in more than 100 countries and territories. It was at this time the company changed its name to Yum! Brands. Given their financial situation and the sheer size of the enterprise, the task of creating massive cultural change was daunting, but that didn't seem to faze David. I loved that attitude. It became clear he was not just interested in creating a Customer Mania culture worldwide, he was going to do it. I would grow to admire his commitment and determination.

I got to spend more time with David six months later, when he asked me to speak at an annual meeting of all the top managers from the company. This time we had a chance for some real give and take and it didn't take long for us to realize we were soul mates. In David's wanting to build a customer-focused company the right way, he was trying to implement everything I have been teaching and writing about for years. And he was doing it in one of the most difficult environments possible.

A GIGANTIC DO-OVER

In golf if you hit a bad shot and say, "I'll take a mulligan," you get to hit again. David Novak uses a similar phrase to depict what his company is up to. He said, "When my daughter, Ashley, was younger and she and her friends made a mistake in their games, they would say, 'I get a do-over.' That's what Yum! is—a gigantic do-over."

The fact that this is a giant do-over makes the task of creating a customer-focused, people-first, performance-driven culture more difficult. It is much easier to implement the concepts I have been teaching over the years when you first start a company than to take an organization that has built a different culture and head it in a new direction. Starting over means winning over skeptics and gaining buy-in for a totally new way of operating.

Yum! is attempting to create a new culture from a group of decentralized companies that actually viewed each other as competitors. Disappointed by the lack of synergy and their overall performance, PepsiCo had come to the decision that it was time to shed even great brands.

While Novak was excited by the challenge, being spun off from PepsiCo made associates anxious. Although everyone knew their combined results were lower than expected, the folks from KFC, Taco Bell, and Pizza Hut still were proud to be a part of PepsiCo, which clearly had credibility and prestige as one of the world's great companies. People in the new acquisitions—Long John Silver's and A&W All American Restaurants—also had uncertain feelings.

Everyone was wondering, "Can they really 'do over' an enormous company made up of firmly entrenched brands?" What would the new company be like? Would benefits go away? Would the company be first class—or coach?

"We've got a real opportunity here," David told me. "How many leaders and teams have the chance to take well-known brands— some that are celebrating their fiftieth anniversary—and start a new company? If we build it the right way, we can create the company of the century."

A COMMON SENSE STRATEGY

As they rebuild their company the right way into a customer-focused enterprise, David Novak and his people are trying to make common sense be common practice. Common sense says that if you consistently treat those who serve customers as if they're the most important people in the company, they will treat customers as if they're the most important people in the world. If a company's people are treated as winners and see themselves as winners, customer satisfaction and profitability come naturally.

Making common sense common practice involves understanding people. In the case of Yum! that means understanding customers, suppliers, franchisees, team members, leaders, and yes, investors—everyone around the globe who is involved or impacted by the organization. With its emphasis on understanding people, one of the things Yum! stands for is:

You Understand Me

RECOGNITION: A UNIVERSAL NEED

The phrase "You Understand Me" means you not only understand my unique needs but also universal needs, such as recognition, that apply across cultures all over the world. David sums it up:

> What we're talking about here is a universal truth. When you put people first, then surround them with processes and disciplines that recognize their efforts, performance will soar. This is becoming a global world. Putting people first doesn't just work in the United States. It's a basic human truth that exists regardless of what religion you are or where you happen to live. In the U.K., China, Malaysia, the Philip-

pines, the Middle East, you name it—recognition drives performance everywhere.

In *The One Minute Manager,* Spencer Johnson (the guy who moved the cheese) and I said that the key to developing people and great organizations is to catch people doing things right and to accentuate the positive. David's commitment to that principle is obvious. He is passionate when he explains that he wants to take recognition and celebration to new levels in building and sustaining exceptional performance around the world.

Foremost among the things that impressed us were David's energy and passion about the company and the business he is in. Just walking into David's office is an experience. Most executives have their company's motto "lamed and framed" on the wall—in this case the motto would be, "We recognize people." But David's *entire wall space* declares the value of recognition. It's completely covered with pictures of people he's honored around the world. David pointed to pictures he'd put on the ceiling when he ran out of wall space.

"The loss-prevention guys are letting me keep those up there as long as they're bolted in so they don't fall and hit someone on the head," he said with a smile.

All that evidence of recognition is not there just for show; it's for *him.* He told us, "I've got the greatest CEO office in the world." He is like a kid in a candy store—so glad to be there.

GETTING HELP

The more I found out about Yum!, the more excited I got about the possibility of documenting their journey. As I said earlier, I'm always looking for good examples of people attempting to practice what I preach, but I had never seen a group of top managers who were interested in "doing the whole thing"—implementing a complete corporate do-over.

When I shared my excitement about their journey being a case study that could help other people and organizations, David and his people got excited, too. Given the size and complexity of the potential assignment, I knew I'd need some help. I asked two of my colleagues, Fred Finch and Jim Ballard, if they would join me on this project. I have known both of them for over thirty years. Fred is a founding associate of The Blanchard Companies and an excellent consultant. Jim is a fine writer and trainer who has worked with me on a number of books, including coauthoring *Whale Done!: The Power of Positive Relationships.*

After Fred, Jim, and I met with David in his office in Louisville, we agreed that he and his people might just pull off rebuilding their company the right way and creating a Customer Mania culture worldwide. But our enthusiasm about the project increased leaps and bounds when David's team said, "Okay, have at it. As long as you don't write a book that's a whitewash." They told us to go anywhere in the company and talk to anybody. "But make sure that anything you write reflects accurately what you find—the good, the bad, and the ugly." That even gave us permission to raise tough questions. This drove us on even more, since we didn't want to be involved in writing a book that amounted to a lot of hoopla. That point was reinforced when David insisted that he didn't want the book to be about him either. Given the egos of CEOs we've run into, that was really impressive.

Knowing that the behavior of top management is always mirrored right down the organization, we began by interviewing senior management people at Yum! corporate, as well as at each of the brands. Focusing on vision, values, and leadership, we got a feeling for what the company believed in, their aspirations, and the direction they were going in their journey. Then we talked to franchise owners, leaders down the line, restaurant managers, and team members, both in the United States and abroad. As the project grew, so did our confidence in the company's commitment to its people.

ORGANIZATION OF THIS BOOK

Over the years I have found that leaders in great organizations, large or small, know how to build a customer-focused company the right way. They do that by leading at a higher level and focusing people's attention on more than making money. They understand the power of a people-first, performance-driven culture and intuitively practice the four key steps to building a company the right way:

Step One: **Set your sights on the right target and vision.**

Step Two: **Treat your customers right.**

Step Three: **Treat your people right.**

Step Four: **Have the right kind of leadership.**

Let me make it clear that when I talk about leaders, in many cases I'm not simply referring to top management. Leadership is an influence process and leaders can be anyone with the opportunity to affect others, for better or worse. A great organization has leaders at all levels.

This book is organized into three parts. The first part contains this introductory chapter and gives a brief history of Yum! Brands. Part II—the main body of the book—zeroes in on the four steps to building a customer-focused company the right way. It consists of four chapters, each representing one of the key steps. The first part of each chapter is labeled Blanchard's Dream and contains my thinking about what it takes to do that step in an ideal way. The second part of each chapter is labeled Yum!'s Reality. This section releases the voices of people throughout Yum!—their leaders, coaches, and associates—and tells their story. It describes how they are using that step to rebuild the right way and accomplish their dream of establishing Customer Mania worldwide. At the end of each chapter is a Scorecard. This is my sense of how well Yum! is doing in each key area compared to the ideal I described in my Dream sections. Part III, Next Steps, explores the challenges they face to keep the momentum going and what they're doing to meet those challenges. The final chapter, "It's Your Choice," will help you make your own decision: Will you go through the "Yum! door" or the "dumb door"?

A BLUEPRINT
FOR DESIRABLE CHANGE

Yum! Brands is not the only company we could have chosen to ex-emplify how to build a customer-focused company, but it is surely the most exciting. Yum! has the most positive, dynamic culture we've ever seen. It is the largest restaurant company in the world, yet the company is dedicated to acting small. Its journey provides a blueprint for desirable change that can be used by all types and sizes of organizations wanting to be more profitable and have more fun achieving their business goals.

The moral of this story is that it's never too late to build a cus-tomer-focused company the right way. While Yum! would be the first to admit it has lots of work to do and has just begun the journey, its leadership is well on its way to taking entrenched brands with checkered pasts and creating a single, exciting culture that's already producing measurable results. As Dave Deno, the company's CFO, likes to say, "All the numbers that should be going up are going up and all the numbers that should be going down are going down." Since its spin-off in 1997 from PepsiCo, Yum! has more than tripled its earnings per share, doubled its return on investment capital and has taken its market capitalization from $3.7 billion to $10 billion. The $4.7 billion of debt Yum! was saddled with is now just $2.1 billion and today the company has an investment-grade quality balance sheet.

We hope you enjoy taking this journey with us. We're sure that regardless of how large or small your company is—whether it's conservative or cutting edge, old or new, whether it involves top level executives or front counter folks—you can build it right by focusing on your customers, too.

KEN BLANCHARD
Spring 2004

CHAPTER 2

A Brief History of Yum! Brands

To APPRECIATE THE MASSIVE NATURE of this do-over, it will be helpful to take a brief look at what the company consists of and where it has come from. Today Yum! Brands is the parent company of KFC, Taco Bell, Pizza Hut, Long John Silver's, and A&W All American Food Restaurants.

FIVE DISTINCTIVE BRANDS

Before we discuss how the company came together, let's take a brief look at each individual brand.

KFC: An American Icon. Based in Louisville, Kentucky, KFC is the world's most popular chicken restaurant chain, specializing in Original Recipe® chicken—made with the same great taste Colonel Harland Sanders created more than a half-century ago—as well as Extra Crispy™, Twister®, and Colonel's Crispy Strips® chicken with home style sides.

Every day, nearly eight million customers are served around the world. KFC's menu also includes more than 300 other products—from a Chunky Chicken Pot Pie in the United States to a salmon sandwich in Japan.

KFC has more than 12,000 restaurants in more than 80 countries and territories around the world. And in quite a few U.S. cities, KFC is teaming up with sister restaurants A&W All American

Food™, Long John Silver's, and Taco Bell to sell products from the popular chains in one convenient location.

Pizza Hut: Entrepreneurial Spirit. The legacy of Pizza Hut began in 1958, when Frank and Dan Carney, two college students from Wichita, Kansas, were approached by a family friend with the idea of opening a pizza parlor. Although the concept was relatively new to many Americans at that time, the brothers quickly saw the potential of this new enterprise.

After borrowing $600 from their mother, they purchased some second-hand equipment and rented a small building on a busy intersection in their hometown. The result of their entrepreneurial efforts was the first Pizza Hut® restaurant, and the foundation for what would become the most successful pizza restaurant company in the world.

Today, Pizza Hut is also the world's largest pizza restaurant company, with nearly 8,000 units in the United States and more than 4,500 units in 141 other countries. The company is the recognized leader of the $37 billion pizza category.

Taco Bell: Mexican Goes Mainstream. Founded by Glen Bell in 1962, the first Taco Bell restaurant was built in Downey, California. As few people outside the Hispanic community knew what a taco was back then, Taco Bell was clearly a concept ahead of its time. But Glen refused to abandon his dream, and he turned his little walk-up restaurant concept into one of the most popular brand names in America.

Today, Taco Bell is the nation's leading Mexican-style quick service restaurant chain, serving tacos, burritos, signature quesadillas, Border Bowls®, nachos, and other specialty items. Over 4.5 million tacos of all varieties are sold in Taco Bell restaurants each day, and Taco Bell serves more than 35 million customers each week in 6,000 restaurants across the United States and in eight countries and two territories around the world.

A&W: The World's Number One Root Beer. A&W Restaurants, Inc., based in Louisville, Kentucky, is the longest running quick service franchise chain in America. Since 1919, A&W All American Food has been serving a signature frosty mug root beer float and All American pure beef hamburgers and hot dogs. There are nearly 800 A&W All American Food outlets in fifteen countries and territories around the world.

Long John Silver's: Quick Service Seafood. Long John Silver's, based in Louisville, Kentucky, is the world's most popular quick service seafood chain, specializing in a variety of seafood items, including batter-dipped fish, chicken, shrimp, and hush puppies. Inspired by Robert Louis Stevenson's classic novel, *Treasure Island,* Long John Silver's was founded in 1969 in response to growing consumer demand for quick service seafood. Today, more than 1,250 Long John Silver's restaurants worldwide serve nearly four million customers each week.

THE BIRTH OF THE CUSTOMER MANIA PHILOSOPHY

Before Yum! was born, the brands were led by a series of pass-through leaders—with mixed results. KFC, in particular, was in trouble in the early nineties.

It Started with KFC. Up to the 1990s KFC's franchisees had enjoyed exclusive rights to their territories. When PepsiCo decided to take back those rights, the franchisee owners got organized and mounted a lawsuit, which dragged on for seven years. Franchisor-franchisee relationships were characterized by divisiveness.

This is the situation David Novak faced in the fall of 1994 when PepsiCo gave him the opportunity to take over KFC. David was a far cry from the typical PepsiCo mold. He didn't wear a jacket and his ties were often askew. He was casual, results-oriented and fun, and people noticed the difference. Most importantly, he listened to people and looked at the facts:

- The franchisee owners control 80 percent of the restaurants.
- If the franchisees don't grow, KFC doesn't grow.
- If the franchisees tank, KFC tanks.
- If the franchisee owners win, KFC wins.

David confronted his new team at its first meeting with this reality. He told them, "Franchisees are a major part of our success. We've been fighting them for years and it hasn't worked, but that's over. We're going to work together—and from now on *we love franchisees.* You may not like franchisees; okay, that's your issue. But from here on out I don't want to hear any more complaints about franchisees or why we can't win with them. No more victimitis. We're going to solve this problem together."

The new chief's next task was to show the franchisees who was in control. He went to nine franchisee regional association meetings and talked to the owners in the same straightforward way. He told them he wasn't going to talk about the lawsuit until "we've worked together and fixed the business and dealt with the customer needs." They liked it when he said, "I love Kentucky Fried Chicken. I don't know the chicken business, but you do. I'd like to know what you would do if you were me."

As David tells it, "I didn't go into my corner office and come out with the answer. I had them break up into groups of eight people, brainstorm lists of suggestions, and come back and tell me what they'd do. Some of them were really mad and when I listened to them I really had to humble myself. They said, 'How do we know you're not just another Pepsi guy who knows squat about the chicken business?' One guy said, 'Son, you'd better be good.' And I said, 'I hope I'm good!'

"Someone said the most powerful way to motivate people is to listen to them. It's true. I listened to them and then took their comments back to my team. We worked it. I started writing 'notes from the desk of David Novak' that said, 'This is what we heard, this is where we're going.' Then I'd get feedback. Gradually we worked together to develop a team strategy."

Simple, huh? You got a problem, ask the people who know. Get them involved; get them to help solve the problem. Once they started to work well with the franchisees and the business started to turn around—i.e., they made their numbers—David and his colleagues sat down with the franchisees and they fixed the lawsuit.

Rallying the Troops at Pizza Hut. In mid-1996 David Novak was asked by PepsiCo to move from KFC to become president of Pizza Hut. At first he refused. When he had assumed leadership of KFC, David had told the staff and franchise owners that he was in for the long haul. A large part of the trust that he had built was based on his commitment not to bail out for another job. PepsiCo's solution was to give him both jobs.

When David took over Pizza Hut, the company was in a state common to many organizations. Call it denial, or simply the inability to step aside and see what they had become. David loves to confront people with what he calls "brutal reality," by which he means the thing that is obvious to everyone that everyone is busy ignoring. So often I find that when a corporation's truth is laid out on the table, upper management goes, "Wow, yeah, you're right on, you got it, man; you're brilliant!" Meanwhile, people in the trenches are going, "Duh."

David's watershed meeting took place in October 1996 in Dallas. All directors and above were brought in, including from the field. Jerry Buss, chief operating officer of Pizza Hut, vividly recalled the Dallas event. "I remember being in the audience," Buss said, "and a lot of us were just shocked by the reality David shared. We had known it before, but basically denied it. David's presentation basically said, 'This is what has been happening to us.' On every major dimension of the business almost imperceptibly over five years, we had been hugely undermining what we were doing.

"The big shock was that we had been shrinking and losing competitiveness. We had been ranking lower and lower in our customers' eyes. We had stopped investing in our restaurant assets. David was saying, 'We used to have *this* amount of sales, and each year they've been eroding.' I remember looking around and seeing all those faces looking like mine must have looked—just pale!"

David's strategy, after taking his audience down, was to bring them back up. He challenged the group, saying they were the leaders, and he needed them to tell him what was going on out there and what they should be doing. His team divided people into groups and took them through an entire day of total involvement. "The energy in that room became magnetic," says Buss. "We talked and talked, getting everything down on flip charts. Then each group presented.

"People began to state the obvious. One marketing guy at my table very eloquently and passionately told us his group had found out 70 percent of our business at the time came through the phone, yet we were doing nothing in terms of building that capability. Suddenly everyone was up out of their seats yelling, 'That's right!' Then others presented, and again people yelled, 'That's right!' You could just feel the energy as we all started realizing, 'Hey, maybe we've got the answers within ourselves!' "

The function of that meeting was to clean the slate and virtually restart the company. It was a high moment, one of those times a gifted leader uses to rally the troops behind his vision. David's message was: "We're in a battle, we're in a fight. We have to turn this around, and we're going to do it." Pizza Hut began to improve its competitiveness and quality. The business was turned around within a year.

THE SPIN-OFF

In 1997, PepsiCo president Roger Enrico and his leadership team decided for strategic reasons to spin off the restaurant group—KFC, Pizza Hut, and Taco Bell. The group had not been performing as well as PepsiCo wanted and he felt that David and his team could do a better job managing the restaurants as a separate, focused restaurant company. Roger also felt PepsiCo could do better as a focused packaged goods company. He had the wisdom to team Novak with the highly regarded Andy Pearson, the former president of PepsiCo and a Harvard Business School professor. Andy, seventy-two at the time, was named chairman and CEO and David, vice chairman and president.

Roger knew Andy's experience and contacts would establish immediate credibility with Wall Street and he would be a great mentor for David. David had actually recommended Andy to Roger to be chairman because he thought he could get to the heart of any business issue faster than any executive he had ever met. David, whom Roger recognized as the company's spiritual leader, would be responsible for driving the day-to-day operations and building a restaurant-focused culture.

The plan worked.

Andy quickly put together one of the most prestigious boards of directors in the world, including such business luminaries as Ron Daniel, vice president, Harvard University and former managing director of McKinsey and Company; James Dimon, president and chief operating officer, J. P. Morgan Chase; Massimo Ferragamo, president and vice chairman, Ferragamo USA, Inc.; Robert Holland,

Jr., former owner and chief executive officer, WorkPlace Integrators; Sidney Kohl, who helped build Kohl's Department Stores; Kenneth Langone, founder, chairman of the board, and chief executive officer, Invemed Associates, LLC, and founder of Home Depot, Inc.; Jackie Trujillo, chairman of the board of Harmon Management Corporation and a member of the Food Service Hall of Fame; Robert Ulrich, chairman and chief executive officer, Target Corporation and Target Stores; Jeanette Wagner, president of Estée Lauder International, Inc; and John Weinberg, senior chairman of Goldman, Sachs & Company.

Right from the beginning, Andy and David hit it off and became not only great partners but best friends. "Think about it," David said. "I was blessed with the opportunity to be coached by one of the great leaders in business history. Andy's a born leader, a born teacher, and from day one he told me his role was to help me become the best possible chief executive officer and build a great company. He definitely walked the talk and has taught me more than I ever imagined. Today, he's the youngest seventy-eight-year-old in the world, still attacking life, still learning and still helping us grow."

When the spin-off took place on October 7, 1997, Pearson and Novak went off site with their new leadership team and established what they called Our Founding Truths. The Founding Truths were established to define the truisms of the business and institutionalize learnings from the past.

Posters were printed with the Truths clearly displayed. The local restaurant managers were asked to become "founders" of the new organization and invited to sign the posters to show their support of the new restaurant-focused philosophy. Team-building activities like these sent a clear message that Pizza Hut, Taco Bell, and KFC were now one company—not three. (The other brands—Long John Silver's and A&W All American Food Restaurants—would be added later.)

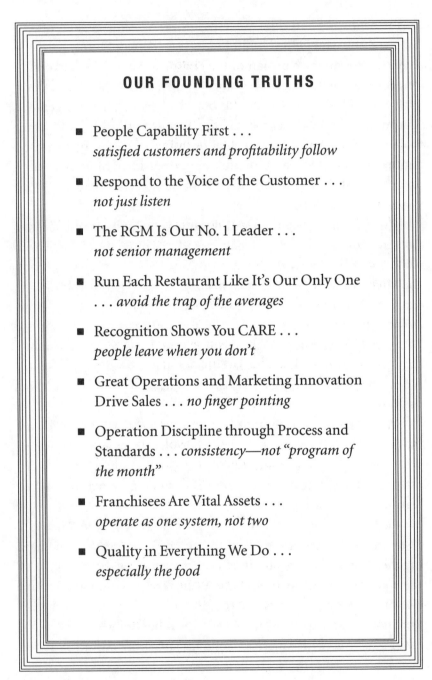

OUR FOUNDING TRUTHS

- People Capability First . . .
  satisfied customers and profitability follow

- Respond to the Voice of the Customer . . .
  not just listen

- The RGM Is Our No. 1 Leader . . .
  not senior management

- Run Each Restaurant Like It's Our Only One
  . . . avoid the trap of the averages

- Recognition Shows You CARE . . .
  people leave when you don't

- Great Operations and Marketing Innovation
  Drive Sales . . . *no finger pointing*

- Operation Discipline through Process and
  Standards . . . *consistency—not "program of
  the month"*

- Franchisees Are Vital Assets . . .
  operate as one system, not two

- Quality in Everything We Do . . .
  especially the food

NAMING YUM!

At the time of the spin-off, the new company did not have a name yet. In the interim, they called it NUCO. When senior vice president of public affairs Jonathan Blum came aboard, one of his first assignments was to come up with a new name. He hired Landor and Associates to help in name generation. Their number one recommendation was the name AMIA. Jonathan said, "It had no real meaning, but it was meant to be a kind, consumer friendly and amiable derivative. I didn't have much experience naming companies, so it sounded okay. We took it up to the senior team. Landor made the presentation and everybody was very polite. They didn't say it was the worst, stupidest name they had ever heard until after the meeting.

"A couple of weeks later, David pulled me aside, put his arm around me, and said, 'Jonathan, since I know you led the charge on the name change, I wanted you to know that we have decided to call the company Tricon. What do you think of that?'

"I said, 'Since you asked me, it sounds clinical—like a nuclear armament company.'

"David smiled and said, 'It stands for our three brands—KFC, Pizza Hut, and Taco Bell—three icons. Tricon—get it?'

"Unfortunately, no one did. It's one of those things that is very clear when you think it up, but I was not sure other people would get it. A while later Patty Sellars from *Fortune* magazine came in to do interviews on our new company. This was the very first article, defining who we are. I got a copy of the article before it came out. The headline read: *Tricon: Great Management, Lousy Name.* I'm beside myself. Here I'm the new head of public affairs, and the first major article that comes out about us is blasting our new name. I didn't know David well then, so I wasn't sure how he would react. So a little anxiously, I walked into his office with the good news/bad news about the *Fortune* article.

"He chuckled and said, 'That's a lot better than *Lousy Management, Great Name!*'

"I thought, *If this is how we're going to go—not take ourselves too seriously and have fun—I'm sticking here for life!*"

In March 2002 Tricon added Long John Silver's and A&W All American Food Restaurants. The strategy behind these acquisitions was to drive global growth by leading the way in multibranding. The executive team believed that multibranding—which combines two brands in one location and therefore doubles the consumer's choices in one restaurant—was the key to future growth. The acquisition of A&W All American Food Restaurants and Long John Silver's was the perfect excuse to change the name. Yum! Brands was the ideal choice, since YUM was already the company's ticker symbol on the New York Stock Exchange. Once the new name was coupled with a new attitude, the do-over was in full swing.

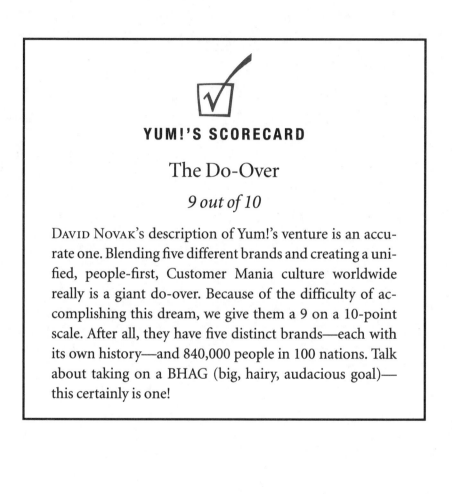

YUM!'S SCORECARD

The Do-Over

9 out of 10

DAVID NOVAK's description of Yum!'s venture is an accurate one. Blending five different brands and creating a unified, people-first, Customer Mania culture worldwide really is a giant do-over. Because of the difficulty of accomplishing this dream, we give them a 9 on a 10-point scale. After all, they have five distinct brands—each with its own history—and 840,000 people in 100 nations. Talk about taking on a BHAG (big, hairy, audacious goal)—this certainly is one!

PART II

＊

How to Build a Customer-Focused Company the Right Way

The Four Steps

CHAPTER 3

STEP ONE
Set Your Sights on the Right Target

THE FIRST STEP IN BUILDING a customer-focused company the right way is to aim for the right target. What follows is my dream of what the right target is. Later in this chapter we'll take a look at what Yum! is aiming at on their journey. Finally, we'll score them on how well they are doing compared to the dream.

BLANCHARD'S DREAM

WALL STREET and the pressures of business today make many people think that the only thing that counts is financial success—being the Investment of Choice. And yet few, if any, businesspeople would want their epitaph to include their company's stock price or profit margin.

In great organizations, everyone's energy is focused on the Triple Bottom Line as the target. If the organization has been built the right way, it will be the Provider of Choice, Employer of Choice, and Investment of Choice. The leaders in great companies believe that people—their customers and associates—are as important as their bottom line. In fact, they know that their customers and their people *create* their bottom line. So many organizations have an either/or philosophy toward results and people. They think they have to choose between the two. But all great organizations I've worked with over the years have the both/and philosophy toward results and people. People—both customers *and* associates—are considered on an equal par with performance. These companies realize that:

**Profit
is the applause
you get for
taking care of
your customers
AND
creating a
motivating environment
for
*your people.***

TAKING CARE OF YOUR CUSTOMERS
(Being the Provider of Choice)

The world has changed in such a way that today the buyer, not the seller, is sitting in the driver's seat. These days, nobody has to convince anybody that the customer is king. Competition is everywhere. People are realizing that their organizations will go nowhere without the loyalty and commitment of their customers. Companies are motivated to change when they discover the new rule:

If you don't take care of your customers, somebody else will.

In *Raving Fans: A Revolutionary Approach to Customer Service,* Sheldon Bowles and I argue that to keep your customers today, you can't be content just to satisfy them; you have to create raving fans. We describe raving fans as customers who are so excited about the way you treat them that they want to tell everyone about you; they become part of your sales force. Let's look at a simple yet powerful example.

What's the most common wake-up call that you get in a hotel in America today? The phone rings at the allotted hour but when you pick it up, there is no one there. At least they got the machine to call your room at the designated hour. The second most common wake-up call greets you with a recording. But again, no one is there. Today if you pick up the phone on a wake-up call and there's a human being on the other end of the line, someone you can actually talk to, you hardly know what to say. A while back I was staying at the Marriott Convention Hotel in Orlando. I asked for a seven o'clock wake-up call. When the phone rang and I picked it up, a woman said, "Good morning, Dr. Blanchard, this is Teresa. It's seven o'clock. It's going to be seventy-five and beautiful in Orlando today, but your ticket says you're leaving. Where are you going?"

Taken aback, I stammered, "I'm going to New York City."

She countered with, "Let me look at the *USA Today* weather map. Oh, no! It's going to be forty degrees and rainy in New York today. Can't you stay another day?"

Now where do you think I want to go when I go to Orlando? I want to go to the Marriott so I can talk to Teresa in the morning! Raving fans are created by companies whose service far exceeds that of the competition, and even customer expectations. These companies routinely do the unexpected, and then enjoy the growth generated by customers who have spontaneously joined their sales force.

CREATING A MOTIVATING ENVIRONMENT FOR YOUR PEOPLE
(Being the Employer of Choice)

You will get little argument today if you tell managers that people are their most important resource. Some even argue that the customer should come second, because without committed and empowered employees, good service can never be provided. You can't treat your people poorly and expect them to treat your customers well.

I had a funny experience recently in a department store that illustrates this point well. I normally shop at Nordstrom's but found myself in a competitor's store. Realizing that I needed to talk to my wife, I asked a salesperson in the men's department if I could use their telephone. "No!" he said.

I said, "You have to be kidding me. You can always use the phone at Nordstrom's."

He said, "Look buddy! They don't let *me* use the phone here. Why should I let you?"

Why exactly are your people so important today? Because these days your organization is evaluated on how quickly it can respond to customer needs and problems. "I'll have to talk to my boss" doesn't cut it anymore. Nobody cares who the boss is. The only people customers care about are the ones who answer the phone, greet them, write up their order, make their delivery, or respond to their complaints. They want top service, and they want it fast. That means you need to create a motivating environment for your people and an organizational structure that is flexible enough to permit them to be the best that they can be.

MAKING YOUR CASH REGISTER GO CA-CHING
(Being the Investment of Choice)

How does all of this impact the bottom line? In two ways. If your profit is a function of revenue minus expenses, you can increase profit either by reducing costs or increasing revenues. Let's look at costs first, because in today's competitive environment, the prize goes to those who can do more with less. More companies are deciding that the only way for them to be financially effective today is to downsize. There's no doubt that some personnel reduction is necessary in large bureaucracies where everyone just had to have an assistant, and then the assistant had to have an assistant. Yet downsizing is an energy drain and it's by no means the only way to manage costs.

There's a growing realization that another effective way to manage cost is to make all of your people your business partners. For instance, in some companies, new people can't get a raise until they can read their company's balance sheet and understand where and how their individual efforts are impacting the company's profit-and-loss statement. When people understand the business realities of how their organization makes money, they are much more apt to roll up their sleeves and help out.

Traditionally, managers have been reluctant to share financial information. But these days, many companies are responding with "open book management" because they realize what large financial gains can be made by sharing previously "sensitive" data. For example, in working with a restaurant company, one of our consulting partners was having a hard time convincing the president of the merits of sharing important financial data with employees. To unfreeze the president's thinking, the consulting partner went to the firm's largest restaurant one night at closing time. Dividing all the employees—cooks, dishwashers, waiters, waitresses, bus people, receptionists—into groups of five or six, he asked them to come to an agreement about the answer to a question: "Of every sales dollar that comes into this restaurant, how many cents do you think fall to the bottom line—money that can be returned to investors as profit or reinvested in the business?"

The least amount any group guessed was forty cents. Several groups guessed seventy cents. In a restaurant, the reality is that if you can keep five cents on the dollar, you get excited—ten cents and you're ecstatic! Can you imagine the attitude among employees toward such things as food costs, labor costs, and breakage if they thought their company was a money machine? After sharing the actual figures, the president was pleased when a chef asked, "You mean, if I burn a steak that costs us six dollars and we sell it for twenty, at a five percent profit margin, we have to sell six steaks for essentially no profit to make up for my mistake?" He already had things figured out.

If you keep your people well-informed and you let them use their brains, you'll be amazed at how they can help manage cost.

What about revenues? If you develop committed and empowered people—Customer Maniacs—who create raving fans, you can't help but increase your revenues. Why? Because every raving fan increases your sales force. That will make your cash register go ca-ching.

Once the leaders of customer-focused companies have established the Triple Bottom Line as the right target—to be the Provider of Choice, Employer of Choice, and Investment of Choice—they are ready to focus everyone's energy on a clear organization vision.

VISION AND DIRECTION: WHERE ARE YOU GOING?

Leadership is about going somewhere. In effective organizations, everyone has a clear sense of where the enterprise is going. They have a compelling vision.

In our book *Full Steam Ahead!*, Jesse Stoner and I contend that there are three parts to a compelling vision. First is *purpose:* what business are you in? Second is a *picture of the future:* what will the future look like when things are running as you planned? Third are *values:* how do you want people to behave when they are working on your purpose and your picture of the future?

Purpose. When Walt Disney started his theme parks, he had a clear purpose—he said they were in the happiness business. That's so much better than having a dry, boring mission statement that couldn't inspire anyone. I was working with a big bank recently. After reading their mission statement I asked them if it would be all right if I kept it by my bedside. If I was having trouble sleeping, I could read their mission statement and immediately be able to go back to sleep.

There's a wonderful organization in Orlando called Give Kids the World that is an implementation operation for the Make-a-Wish Foundation. Kids who are dying who always wanted to go to Disney World or SeaWorld or other attractions in Orlando can get a chance through Give Kids the World. Over the years they have brought more than 50,000 families to Orlando for a week at no cost to them. They think having a sick child is a family issue, therefore everyone gets to come to Orlando. When you ask them what business they are in, they tell you they're in the memory business—they want to create memories for these kids.

When I was there one time I passed a man who was cutting the grass. I thought I would test how widely understood this mission was, so I stopped and asked him, "What business are you in here at Give Kids the World?"

He smiled and said, "We make memories."

"How do you make memories?" I asked. "You just cut the grass."

He said, "I certainly don't make memories by continuing to cut the grass if a family comes by. You can always tell who the sick kid is, so I ask that youngster whether he or she or a brother or sister want to help me with my chores."

Isn't that a wonderful attitude? It keeps him focused on servicing the folks who come to Give Kids the World.

Picture of the Future. When it came to his theme parks, Walt Disney's picture of the future was that when guests left the parks, they would have the same smile on their face as when they entered six, eight, ten, or twelve hours earlier. "Keep our guests smiling" was the rallying call.

At Give Kids the World, their picture of the future is that in the last week of the lives of youngsters who have been there, they will still be laughing and talking to their families about their time in Orlando.

Values. The third part of a compelling vision is values. Values drive people's behavior when they are working on your purpose and your picture of the future. Few organizations have operational values, and those that do usually make one or two common mistakes. First, they have too many values—eight, ten, or twelve. Our research shows that people can't handle more than three or four values if the values are to guide their behavior. The second mistake is that organizations seldom rank-order their values. Life is about value conflicts. If values are simply listed and people can pick or choose whatever value they want, it's a setup for them to practice situational ethics.

At the Disney theme parks they have four rank-ordered values: safety, courtesy, the show, and efficiency. Why is safety the highest-ranked value? Walt Disney knew that if guests were carried out of one of his parks on a stretcher, they would not have the same smile on their face leaving the park as they had when they entered six, eight, ten, or twelve hours earlier.

The second-ranked value, courtesy, is all about the friendly attitude you expect at a Disney park. Why is it important to know that it's the number two value? Suppose one of their cast members is answering a guest question in a friendly, courteous manner, and a scream is heard that's not coming from the roller coaster. If that cast member is going to act according to the rank-ordered values, he will excuse himself as quickly and politely as possible and race toward the scream. Why? Because the number one value just called. If the values were not rank-ordered and the cast member was enjoying the interaction with the guest, she might say, "They're always yelling in the park," and not move in the direction of the scream. Later somebody could come to that cast member and say, "You were the closest to the scream. Why didn't you move?" The response could be, "I was dealing with our courtesy value." You see, life is a series of value conflicts. There are going to be times when you can't do two values at the same time.

Having a set of operating values is very important in an organization. In companies that don't have any, everybody brings their own values to work. And today—given the cultural diversity of our population—that could become confusing.

THE IMPORTANCE OF VISION

Clear vision is all-important. It tells people—both internally and externally—who you are (purpose), where you're going (picture of the future), and what will guide your journey (values). Once clear vision is set, the established goals are placed in context. Goals tell people what they should focus on right now. After all, good performance starts with clear goals.

The traditional hierarchical pyramid is well suited for this visionary/direction aspect of leadership. Clear vision and direction starts with top management and must be communicated throughout the organization by the leadership. People look to their formal leaders for vision and direction. While top management should involve experienced people in shaping direction, the ultimate *responsibility* for having a vision remains with the higher-ups and cannot be delegated to others. If an enterprise is to be effective, people throughout an organization must be *responsive* to this vision.

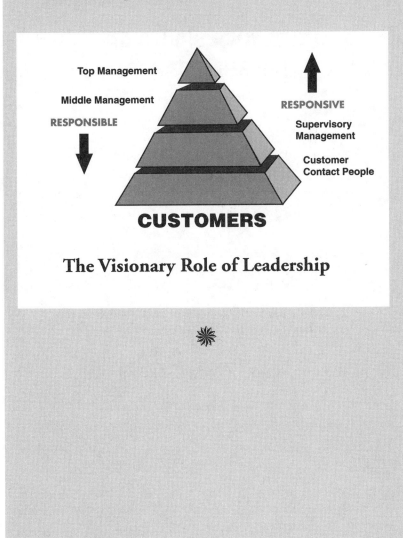

The Visionary Role of Leadership

SET YOUR SIGHTS ON THE RIGHT TARGET

SUMMARY STATEMENTS

A customer-focused company with its sights set on the right target would:

- Be the *Provider of Choice* and take care of its customers.

- Be the *Employer of Choice* and create a motivating environment for its people.

- Be the *Investment of Choice* and have the cash register go ca-ching.

- Have an agreed-upon, compelling *vision.*

YUM!'S REALITY: SETTING THEIR SIGHTS HIGH

THE MORE WE TALKED with people at Yum!, the more we observed that they have the right target. The company is aiming high. Not only does its vision and direction focus on the Triple Bottom Line (being the Provider of Choice, Employer of Choice, and Investment of Choice) but its success formula—*People Capability First . . . Satisfied Customers and Profitability Follow*—emphasizes the right priorities: its people and customers, and then profits.

PURPOSE: WHO ARE THEY?

Yum! doesn't merely have a purpose, it has a *passion*. And that's what they call it.

Our Passion

Customer Mania . . . act as one system to put a Yum! on customers' faces around the world.

Pete Bassi, chairman of Yum! Restaurants International, described the Passion Statement this way: "The word *Yum!* has a personal and positive connotation. When something tastes good, you say, 'Yum!' and there's a smile on your face. But when we say, 'Put a Yum! on everyone's face,' we mean more than preparing and serving great food to people. We also mean making them feel good about their total experience of coming into one of our restaurants. It translates all around the world. It also says we're a fun, different kind of company."

Putting a Yum! on people's faces includes not only attending to customers but also fulfilling the needs of employees, franchisees and, of course, investors. Peter Hearl, president of Pizza Hut and an international veteran, explains, "The deeper, cultural meaning of Yum! is that, both inside and outside the organization, we are committed to developing lasting and meaningful relationships with people. For our employees worldwide, that feeling of being understood is essential. That's what *You Understand Me* is all about.

"Here the smile on your face is the result of feeling a part of this organization and knowing you can make a difference. You get up every day and go to work knowing it's an emotional, exciting, fun, rewarding, challenging, and spirited-feeling place to be."

PICTURE OF THE FUTURE: WHERE ARE THEY GOING?

The picture of the future for Yum!'s leaders is big and bright. They aspire to be among the top ten companies to work for, the top ten most admired companies, and the best restaurant company in the world. If a quick service food company has aspirations this colossal, the leadership knows they'd better have a breathtaking culture. They understand an important truth:

The most powerful way to produce desired change in an organization is to impact its culture.

What is culture? It's a shared system of what's meaningful. It's what people pay attention to, how they act and what they value. That's what Yum! wants to have—an awesome culture with a people-first, performance-driven foundation. The key is not either people *or* results, it is both people *and* results.

The company's commitment to *and* thinking allows them to envision a radically different culture. Paying attention *first* to universal human needs (such as the need to be trusted and believed in, to do one's best, to learn to improve, to be recognized and rewarded) drives peak performance. The fact that these needs are universal means the culture can spread across the apparent barriers of language, ethnicity, and race and be perpetuated throughout the world.

The following stories capture the essence of the culture the company is trying to create. They're about two people: Mario Garcia, a restaurant general manager (RGM), and his mentor, Jane Lanza, an area coach for Taco Bell on Long Island in New York State. The words are Mario's and Jane's, not ours, and they are a testimony to Yum!'s positive culture.

MARIO GARCIA, RGM, TACO BELL

I came to the United States from El Salvador in 1990 when I was nineteen years old. Two of my relatives had already come here and they arranged and paid for my way here along with two of my other relatives. I had family and friends on Long Island, so that's where I ended up. I came to the United States to find work, make a living, and help my family back in El Salvador.

My cousin said I should put in an application at Taco Bell. I didn't think that would work out, since I spoke very little English, but I decided to try. At the restaurant I met Jane Lanza, who was the restaurant general manager (RGM) at that time. She said she had no available hours, but if I would come in on the weekend for two hours each day and clean the parking lot she would help me out.

I said yes, and within a couple of weeks I was working forty hours a week. I guess Jane thought I was a reliable worker. It helped that there were a lot of Spanish-speaking people working in the restaurant and they gave a lot of help and support. I worked hard and during breaks I studied English. Pretty quickly I could talk in what we called Taco English—enough English to be able to work well in the restaurant.

Jane helped me a lot. She gave me opportunities to learn new things. After a year or so I was promoted to shift supervisor. That was a big deal for me. I wouldn't even have tried if Jane hadn't kept helping me and telling me I could do it. Within two years I was promoted to assistant unit manager in another restaurant. I had to learn a lot about how to handle people and what it takes to run a restaurant. I had to learn how to lead people who used to be my team members. That was tough.

During the next few years I worked in six different restaurants and became a senior assistant manager. I had built up enough experience and skills that I was promoted to restaurant general manager of a multibrand—a combination Taco Bell and Pizza Hut Express—a new kind of restaurant the company was beginning to build on Long Island.

I wasn't sure that I could handle it, but Jane Lanza had been promoted to area coach and my new position was going to be in her area. That made me feel a lot better about the new job because I knew Jane would help me. After a couple of months she told me I was leaning on her too much. I began to take care of things by myself and with the help of my team. Jane was always available if I needed her. At the end of my first year I had 132 percent growth in year-over-year store sales, which was best in our region.

One of the things I like best about my job is helping other people develop, just like Jane helped me. It really makes me feel good to see them get ahead. I also really enjoy getting my people involved in what's going on in the restaurant.

JANE LANZA, TACO BELL AREA COACH

The core of the RGM job is developing people. If you don't develop your people, bad things happen. Even if you're a great leader, you can't be in the restaurant all the time. What really matters in a store is not what happens when you're there, but what happens when you're not there. So you have to develop your people and build them into a team that enjoys working there.

I always say you have to create a home feeling where people enjoy their work, where they work hard and also have fun, enjoy each other, and especially enjoy serving customers. If you don't like serving cus-

tomers, you are in the wrong job—and that goes for every team member and leader in the restaurant. This is a very complicated job, but it is a lot easier if you have developed your people.

Currently, about 90 percent of our team members are Spanish-speaking immigrants; there was less at that time, but not much. If they don't speak English, it's hard to provide opportunities for empowerment. I would start out with an individual and their first response was, 'No, I can't do that.' But when you took the time and coached, supported, and provided recognition for them, they went for it. They surprised themselves, just as Mario did.

You can tell right away when an RGM has built a great restaurant organization. It's not what you see, it's what you feel. Being in a good restaurant produces a feeling. There is no sense of tension. Even before you have any direct contact with a team member, you get a feeling for what this restaurant is like. It's in the details. If there's something spilled on the floor, someone notices and takes care of it without being told. Everywhere you look, they are taking the initiative. If team members feel like the restaurant is like their home, then they treat it like their home.

We used to hire people from the outside. Now we promote from within, based on job performance. My experience says that the best people are the ones we develop from within. Mario is an excellent example of that.

These testimonies are characteristic of a people-first culture dedicated to producing results. Jane's supportive relationship with Mario and Mario's support of his people as he runs a top-performing restaurant typify the company's dedication to people *and* results.

THE YUM! DYNASTY

What is the company's strategy for creating more Mario and Jane stories throughout the organization? It's the Yum! Dynasty Model—their picture of the future.

In many organizations the word *dynasty* would be associated with power amassed under a single ruler, with personal glorification and a succession of heirs to perpetuate the family name. CEO David Novak is indeed concerned about what the company will be like for generations to come, but the Yum! Dynasty is not there to pay homage to the company's founding fathers. It's a vision of a shared future, lasting and bright. The idea behind the word *dynasty* is to fire people's minds with purpose, to give them a sense of being a part of an ongoing journey—a journey with a company flexible enough to adapt to change, yet solid enough to ensure long-term sustainability.

The company has set its sights on the Dynasty Model as the right target. Their mission statement—Our Passion—reinforces the spirit of Customer Mania. It's both a statement of what they want everyone in the organization to be—Customer Maniacs—and a way of life to address customer service. The Formula for Success identifies the core notion of their culture: people capability first and then results—customer satisfaction and profitability—will follow. The roles of the leaders are identified and the company's goals are captured in five major strategies. The *How We Work Together* principles and the franchisee pact (the mutually agreed upon commitments that Yum! and the franchisees have signed up for) are the foundation upon which everything else rests. What really makes this Dynasty Model work is adherence to the *How We Work Together* principles, which essentially are the company's values.

CORE VALUES:
WHAT WILL GUIDE THEIR JOURNEY?

Values are about how people will behave when they are living up to the purpose and the picture of the future that leaders have communicated. Gregg Dedrick, president of KFC and former chief people officer for Yum!, shared with us how the company came up with the values that would guide and drive the organization.

THE YUM! DYNASTY MODEL

Our Passion

Customer Mania . . .
act as one system to put a Yum!
on customers' faces around the
world

Our Formula for Success

People Capability First . . .
satisfied customers and
profitability follow

How We Lead

1. Be a Customer Maniac
2. Know and Drive the Business
3. Build, Inspire, and Align Teams

How We Win

Be the best at providing customers branded
restaurant choices . . . multibranding great brands

| 1. Run great restaurants | 2. Differentiate the brands in everything we do | 3. Drive global expansion | 4. Lead the way in multi-branding | 5. Convert cash flow into high value |

How We Work Together

Our *How We Work Together* Leadership Principles
Our Franchisee Partnership Pact

"Basically," said Dedrick, "everything we did early on was based on a symbolic model. We asked: What's our strategy? What's our structure to support it? And what is the culture—the values that are going to drive and hold it all together? We made it the job of the leadership team to collect information in each of these areas and shape and communicate that to the organization. We were continually in the process of getting feedback about what was working and what wasn't."

Early on, Novak and his cofounders began a relentless benchmarking of top-performing companies in a variety of industries. They also studied what great restaurant general managers did and what made their own best restaurants tick. The team concluded that great operations outside and inside their business had a customer focus and an unflagging adherence to eight key operating principles. They named these principles *How We Work Together* and declared that adherence to them by all associates was required to run a great restaurant.

The company's vision—the target they're aiming at—consists of their Passion Statement, the Yum! Dynasty Model, and their *How We Work Together* principles. Yum!'s president of Greater China, Sam Su—who oversees China, Taiwan, and Hong Kong—sums up the importance of Yum!'s vision and direction:

At PepsiCo, they had a very results oriented culture—big guys doing big things. But there was no real focus or expertise on the restaurant business. I think the spin-off was the greatest thing that could have happened to Yum! The people who wanted to be at Pepsi stayed, and the people with passion for the restaurant business joined us. And we started to form a future of our own. Because we're now one business I think we're much more focused and sharper. All these things—our passion, dynasty, the *How We Work Together* principles—helped us understand and execute what is criti-

THE *HOW WE WORK TOGETHER* (HWWT) PRINCIPLES (YUM!'S VALUES)

Customer Mania

We not only listen and respond to the voice of the customer, we are obsessed to go the extra mile to make our customers happy.

Belief in People

We believe in people, trust in positive intentions, encourage ideas from everyone and actively develop a workforce that is diverse in style and background.

Recognition

We find reasons to celebrate the achievements of others and have fun doing it.

Coaching and Support

We coach and support each other.

Accountability

We do what we say, we are accountable, we act like owners.

Executional Excellence

We beat year-ago results by continuously improving and innovating. We follow through with daily intensity.

Positive Energy

We execute with positive energy and intensity—we hate bureaucracy and all the nonsense that comes with it.

Teamwork

We practice team together, team apart after productive conflict.

cal to be successful in our restaurant business. It's all about people first and responding to customers.

China is the company's greatest example of the power of vision. Initially, there was skepticism that Yum!'s high-energy recognition culture would play in conservative China. Yet Sam Su saw the vision, embraced it, and has taken it to a whole new level. Since the beginning of the spin-off, profits in China have gone from $15 million to $150 million and the China group recently celebrated the opening of their one thousandth KFC.

YUM!'S SCORECARD

Setting Its Sights on the Right Target

8 out of 10

WHEN IT COMES to having a vision, Yum! gets a score of 8. You might say, "Sure, their purpose and picture of the future are clear, but you said a company should only have three or four values, and they have eight! And you said the values should be rank-ordered, yet the company's leadership doesn't say that their HWWT principles are rank-ordered."

I have several responses to those charges. First, I did tell Novak and his key leaders they should have only a few values, but they have been doing such a great job cascading them throughout the organization, they thought I was wrong in this case. In fact, Aylwin Lewis, their COO, told me I was crazy because the HWWT principles were already established and working. Hearing about the universal acceptance and knowledge of these principles, I backed off. In terms of rank-ordering their values, Yum! does that in their own way. Since their goal is to create a Customer Mania culture and the three key elements driving that are Belief in People, Recognition, and Coaching and Support, these are primary. Accountability, Excellence, Positive En-

(continued on following page)

(continued from previous page)

ergy, and Teamwork, while important, are not as highly ranked in everybody's mind as the first four.

My conclusion is that even though they have not followed my benchmarking to the T, they should still get an 8. In terms of clarity, these people know who they are, where they're going and what will guide their journey. What keeps them from perfection—a 10—is that they haven't driven the vision down through the roofs yet to the restaurant level. So they still have some work to do in making the vision universally understood and acted upon where it really counts—at the restaurant and with their customers.

I'll never forget having lunch once with Max DePree, the legendary chairman of Herman Miller. I asked him what his main role was as CEO of this great company. He said, "My emphasis is on the vision. I have to be like a third-grade teacher. I have to say it over and over and over and over again, until people get it right, right, right."

Here's hoping that Yum! can continue to recruit a lot of third-grade teachers who will get the message to everyone, everywhere.

CHAPTER 4

STEP TWO
Treat Your Customers the Right Way

THE SECOND STEP IN BUILDING a customer-focused company is to treat your customers right. While everybody seems to know that, few organizations are creating raving fans—customers who want to brag about them. Here is my strategy.

BLANCHARD'S DREAM

IF YOU WANT TO CREATE RAVING FANS, you don't just announce it. You have to plan for it—you have to visualize it. What kind of experience do you want your customers to have as they interact with every aspect of your organization?

VISUALIZE YOUR DREAM

Sheldon Bowles, who coauthored *Raving Fans* with me in 1993, was one of the founders of a full-service gasoline chain in Western Canada called Domo Gas. Back in the 1970s, when everybody was going to self-service gasoline stations, Sheldon knew that if people had a choice they certainly wouldn't choose to come to a gas station. Therefore, if they came, they wanted to get in and out as quickly as possible. The customer service vision that Sheldon and his cofounders imagined was an Indianapolis 500 pit stop. They dressed all their attendants in red jump suits. When a customer would drive into one of their stations, two or three people would run out of the hut and race toward the car. As quickly as possible, they would look under the hood, clean the windshield, and pump the gas. In a California station that got excited about the concept, they would give the customer a cup of coffee and a newspaper, ask him or her to step out of the car, and dust-bust the interior. As customers pulled away, each received a flyer that said: "P.S. We also sell gas."

I love the Moments of Truth concept that Jan Carlzon used to create a customer-focused culture when he was president of the Scandinavian Airlines System (SAS):

> "A Moment of Truth is anytime a customer comes in contact with anyone in our organization in a way that they can get an impression. How do we answer the phone? How do we check people in? How do we greet them on our planes? How do we interact with them during flights? How do we handle baggage claim? What happens when a problem occurs?"

Great customer service organizations analyze every key interaction they have with customers and determine how they would like to have that scenario played out. One of the ways to think about that is to suppose that the word has gotten out about how fabulously you are serving customers. There are ecstatic customers running all over the place, bragging about you. A well-known television station gets word of this and decides they want to send a crew in to film what is going on in your organization. Who would you want them to talk to? What would your people tell them? What would these folks be seeing?

Creating raving fans starts with a picture, an image of what kind of experience you want your customers to have. Analyzing your Moments of Truth for each department and deciding how you want them played out is a good start.

LISTENING TO THE CUSTOMER

After you decide what you want to have happen, it's important to find out what your customers want to have happen. What would make their experience with you better? Ask them! But ask them in a way that stimulates an answer. For example, how many times have you been eating at a restaurant when the restaurant manager comes over and says to you, "How is everything tonight?" Isn't your usual response, "Fine"? That gives restaurant managers no information. I don't know why they waste their time. What would be better for them to say is, "Excuse me. I'm the restaurant manager. I wonder if I could ask you one question. Is there anything that we could have done differently tonight that would have made your experience with us better?" That question invites an answer. If they say "No" you can follow it up with a sincere "Are you sure?"

You have to be creative in discovering what customers want. And when they tell you, you have to listen without being defensive. One reason people get uptight when they listen to customers is because they think they always have to do what the customer wants them to do. They don't understand that there are two parts of listening. The first is, as author Steve Covey says, "Seek first to understand." In other words, listen for understanding. Try saying, "That's interesting. Tell me more. Could you be more specific?"

The second aspect of listening is to decide if you want to do anything about what you've heard. That has to be separated from the understanding aspect of listening. And it is important to realize that deciding does not have to be done right after you understand what the person is suggesting. You can do it later, when you have some time to think about it or talk it over with others. Realizing you have time to think it over will make you less defensive and a better listener. After listening to understand, then you can decide what you want to do about what you've heard.

In the mall recently I saw an example of defensive listening. I was walking behind a woman who had an eight- or nine-year-old son. As they walked past the sporting goods store, the kid looked over and saw a beautiful red bicycle outside the store. He stopped in his tracks and said to his mother, "Boy, would I like a bike like that." His mother nearly went crazy and started screaming: "I can't believe it! I just got you a new bike for Christmas! Here it is March and you already want another one! I'm not going to get you another $%&*^! thing!" I thought she was going to nail this kid's head into the cement. Sadly, she didn't distinguish the need to separate listening for understanding from deciding. If she had said to the kid, "Honey, what do you like about that bike?" he might have said, "See those streamers coming out of the handlebars? I really like them." And those streamers could have been a cheap birthday present. After listening to what he liked about the bike, the mother could have said, "Honey, why do you think I can't get you that new bike?" The kid was no idiot. I bet he would have said, "I just got a new one for Christmas."

Listening without being defensive is also helpful if you make mistakes with customers. Defending what you've done will only irritate them. When they are upset, all customers want is to be heard. In fact, research has shown that if you listen to a complaining customer in a nondefensive, attentive way and then ask, "Is there any way we could win back your loyalty?" eight out of ten times the customer will say, "You've already done it. You listened to me."

If a customer makes a good suggestion or is upset about something that makes sense to change, you can add that suggestion to your customer service picture. For example, recently I got a letter from a man who owns three quick service restaurants in the Midwest. Some of his elderly customers suggested that during certain parts of the day he should have tablecloths on the tables and have people take their order at the table and deliver the food to where they are sitting. After thinking about it, he realized it was a pretty good idea. Now, between three and five in the afternoon the tables have tablecloths, candles, and the people behind the counter come out and wait on the customers. The elderly are pouring in to his restaurants during those hours.

When you put together what you want your customers to experience with what they want to have happen, you will have a pretty complete picture of your desired customer service experience.

LIVING YOUR CUSTOMER SERVICE VISION

Now that you have a clear picture of the experience you want your customers to have that will satisfy them, delight them, and put smiles on their faces, you have to figure out how to get your people excited about this vision and willing to make it happen.

As I emphasized in Chapter 3, Set Your Sights on the Right Target, the responsibility for setting the vision and direction rests with the top of the hierarchy. And that responsibility includes establishing your customer service vision. Once that vision is set and people are committed to it, implementation begins.

Implementation is all about equipping people throughout the organization to act as owners of the vision and direction. It is during implementation where most organizations get into trouble. The traditional pyramid is kept alive and well, leaving customers uncared for at the bottom of the hierarchy. All the energy in the organization moves up the hierarchy as people try to please and be responsive to their bosses. Now the bureaucracy rules and policies and procedures carry the day. This leaves unprepared and uncommitted customer-contact people to quack like ducks.

Wayne Dyer, the great personal growth teacher, said years ago there are two kinds of people in life: ducks and eagles. Ducks act like victims and go, "Quack! Quack! Quack!" Eagles, on the other hand, take the initiative and soar above the crowd. As a customer, you can always identify a bureaucracy if you have a problem and are confronted by ducks who quack: "It's our policy. I didn't make the rules—I just work here. Do you want to talk to my supervisor? Quack! Quack! Quack!"

Let me give you an example. I'm a trustee emeritus at Cornell University. A while back I was heading to a meeting in Ithaca, New York, the small upstate town where Cornell is located. I wanted to rent a car that I could drop off at Syracuse, which was about an hour and a half away. You have probably traveled enough to know that if you drop a car off at a different place than where you rented it, they charge you a big drop-off fee. You can avoid that drop-off fee if they have a car that came from where you are going. So I asked the woman behind the counter, "Do you have a Syracuse car?"

She said, "You're lucky. I happen to." Then she went into the computer and prepared my contract.

I'm not a particularly detail-oriented person, but as I was signing my contract I saw a $75 drop-off fee out of the corner of my eye. I said, "What's that $75 drop-off fee?"

She said, "I didn't do it. Quack! Quack!"

I said, "Who did?"

She said, "The computer. Quack! Quack!"

I said, "How do we tell the computer it was wrong?"

"I don't know. Quack! Quack!"

I said, "Why don't you just cross it out?"

She said, "I can't. My boss will kill me. Quack! Quack!"

"You mean I have to pay a $75 fee because you have a mean boss?"

"I remember one time—quack! quack!—my boss let me cross it out."

"When was that?"

"When the customer worked for Cornell. Quack! Quack!"

I said, "That's great. I'm on the board of trustees of Cornell!"

She asked, "What does the board do? Quack! Quack!"

"We can fire the president."

"What's your employee number? Quack! Quack!"

"I don't have one."

"What am I going to do? Quack! Quack!"

It took me twenty minutes of psychological counseling to

get out of this drop-off fee. I used to get angry at these frontline people, but I don't anymore. Why? It's not really their fault. Who do you think this woman worked for, a duck or an eagle? Obviously, a duck. If she worked for an eagle, the eagle would eat the duck. We call the supervisory duck the head mallard, because they just quack at a higher level. They tell you all the rules and regulations and laws that apply to your situation. Who do you think the supervisory duck works for? Another duck, who works for whom? Another duck, who works for whom? Another duck. And who sits at the top of the organization? A great big duck. Have you ever been hit by an eagle turd? Obviously not, because they soar above the crowd. It's the ducks that make all the mess.

How do you create an organization where ducks are busted and eagles can soar? The traditional pyramid hierarchy must be turned upside down, so the frontline people who are closest

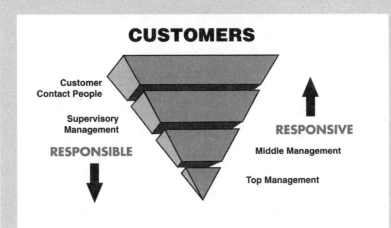

The Implementation Role of Leadership

to the customers are at the top. Here they can be *responsible—* able to respond to their customers. In this scenario, leaders *serve* and are *responsive* to the needs of people, training and developing them to soar like eagles so they can accomplish established goals and live according to the vision they have of the customer experience.

If the leaders in an organization do not respond to the needs and desires of their people, these folks will not take good care of their customers. But when the frontline customer-contact people are treated as responsible owners of the vision, they can soar like eagles and create raving fans rather than quack like ducks.

Permitting People to Soar. A friend of mine experienced an eagle incident when he went to Nordstrom's one day to get some perfume for his wife. The woman behind the counter said, "I'm sorry but we don't sell that perfume in our store. But I know where I can get it in the mall. How long are you going to be in our store?"

"About thirty minutes," he said.

"Fine, I'll go get it, bring it back, gift wrap it, and have it ready for you when you leave." This woman literally left Nordstrom's, went to another store, got the perfume that he wanted, came back to Nordstrom's, and gift wrapped it. You know what she charged him? The same price that she had paid at the other store. So they didn't make any money on the deal but what did they make? A raving fan.

I had a beautiful example of the different experiences you can have with organizations depending on whether they are duck ponds or they permit people to soar like eagles. A while back I was heading to the airport for a trip that was going to take me to four different cities during the week. As I approached the airport, I realized that I had forgotten my license and didn't have a passport with me, either. Not having time to go back home to get them and make the flight, I had to be creative.

Only one of my books has my picture on the cover, and that is *Everyone's a Coach,* which I wrote with Don Shula. So when I got to the airport I ran into the bookstore and luckily, they had a copy of our book. Fortunately, the first airline I had to go to was Southwest Airlines. As I was checking my bag at the curb, the porter asked to see my identification. I said, "I feel badly. I don't have a driver's license or a passport. But will this do?" And I showed him the cover of the book. He shouted out, "The man knows Shula! Put him in first class!" (Of course, Southwest doesn't have first class.) Everybody out by the curb check-in started to high-five me. I was like a hero. Then one of the baggage handlers said, "Why don't I go in the terminal with you? I know the folks in security. I think I can get you through there, too."

Why did that happen? Herb Kelleher, who founded Southwest, not only wanted to give his customers the lowest possible price, but he wanted to give them the best possible service. He set the whole organization up to empower everyone—right to the frontline baggage check folks—with power to make decisions, use their brains and be Customer Maniacs, so they could create raving fans. Kelleher (who has recently retired and turned over the presidency to his former executive assistant, Colleen Barrett) believed that policies should be followed but that people could use their brains in interpreting them. Why do they ask for identification at the airport? To make sure that the person getting on the plane is the same person as the name on the ticket. That was an easy decision for the Southwest Airlines' frontline person.

Wallowing in a Duck Pond. The next airline I had to go to before my office could overnight my driver's license was an airline that is in financial trouble. The baggage handler at the curbside check-in looked at the book and said, "You've got to be kidding me. You'd better go to the ticket counter."

When I showed the book to the woman at the ticket counter, she said, "You'd better talk to my supervisor." I was moving up the hierarchy fast. I thought maybe pretty soon I was going to get to the mayor and then finally to Governor Arnold Schwarzenegger. Quack! Quack! Quack! In the troubled airline, the hierarchy was alive and well. All the energy was moving away from pleasing the customers and moving toward serving the hierarchy—and following the policies, procedures, rules, and regulations to the letter.

Giving Your People Wings. Horst Schulze, one of the founders of the Ritz-Carlton Hotels, retired a few years ago as president and CEO. During Horst's reign, after orientation and extensive training, every employee was given a $2,000 discretionary fund that they could use to solve a customer problem without checking with anyone. They didn't even have to tell their boss. Horst loved to collect stories about people really using this empowerment to make a difference.

One of my favorites is about a businessman who was staying at one of the Ritz-Carlton properties in Atlanta. That day he had to fly from Atlanta to Los Angeles and then from Los Angeles to Hawaii, because the next day at one o'clock he was making a major speech to his international company. He was a little disorganized as he was leaving. On his way to the airport he discovered that he'd left behind his laptop computer, which contained all the Power Points he needed for his presentation.

He tried to change his flights, but couldn't. So he called the Ritz-Carlton and said, "This is the room I was in, this is where my computer was. Have Housekeeping get it and overnight it to me. They have to guarantee delivery by ten o'clock tomorrow morning, because I need it for my one o'clock speech."

The next day Schulze was wandering around the hotel, as he often did. When he got to Housekeeping he said, "Where's Mary?" Her coworkers said, "She's in Hawaii." Horst said, "Hawaii? What's she doing in Hawaii?"

He was told, "A guest left a computer in his room and he needs it for a speech today at one o'clock—and Mary doesn't trust overnight carrier services anymore." Now you might think that Mary went for a vacation, but she came back on the next plane. And what do you think was waiting for her? A letter of commendation from Horst and high fives around the hotel. That's really empowering people and giving them wings. You might say, "Blanchard, is this story really true?" The answer is yes, but let me tell you something that's important to remember. If you create an environment where the customers rule and your people can use their brains to take care of customer needs, stories like this become commonplace, even legendary. Everyone who tells these stories—including your customers—will add to them.

TREAT YOUR CUSTOMERS THE RIGHT WAY

SUMMARY STATEMENTS

If you want to create raving fans—customers who want to brag about the way you treat them—you have to:

- Determine what kind of experience you want your customers to have.

- Listen to what your customers want and see if it makes sense to include their suggestions in your vision.

- Implement your customer service vision by inverting the traditional hierarchal pyramid so your customer contact people are at the top, ready to soar like eagles and serve.

YUM!'S REALITY:
CREATING CUSTOMER MANIA

How DOES YUM! get its mission to create Customer Mania off its wall plaque and into action—from Louisville to Singapore? By turning everyone into Customer Maniacs—people who are passionate about going the extra mile for the customer. The more we talked with people at Yum!, the more we felt that Customer Mania was indeed starting to be a shared passion.

Customer Mania
We not only listen and respond to the voice of the customer, we are obsessed to go the extra mile to make our customers happy.

President and chief multibranding and operating officer Aylwin Lewis says, "It's a calling. Unless you're passionate about serving food to masses of people in such a way that it puts a Yum! on their faces, you might as well forget it. Leaders are the guardians at the gate. It has to be in the leaders first, and that in turn dictates whom you hire and whom you promote. You can't get promoted here unless you can demonstrate how you are a Customer Maniac, what your personal recognition award is, and how you live the *How We Work Together* principles."

WHAT PRODUCES CUSTOMER MANIACS?

Customer Maniacs have an intense enthusiasm for serving others. They get joy from making customers happy. Customer Mania starts at the leadership level; it's a natural extension of Yum!'s cascading principle. From the outset—and from the top—the *How We Work Together* values have been rigorously cascaded throughout the organization. Customer Mania is that cascading principle extended out to customers.

Taco Bell President and chief concept officer Emil Brolick says, "The logic goes: If restaurant people receive training and coaching in their work skills and support and recognition when they perform well, they experience personal development and feel much better about themselves. Then they can be high-performing Customer Maniacs who give customers extraordinary care. If you have Customer Maniacs, sales and profits will emerge. It's an elevating spiral: If you want customers' emotional attachment, you've got to work back from it to the people who are serving them."

LISTENING TO THE CUSTOMERS

Yum! Restaurants International mounted a major research effort to determine—from the customers—what they wanted. The result was CHAMPS. The company did not just make assumptions about what customers wanted. CHAMPS is an acronym for the things the company identified that were important from the customers' point of view. CHAMPS stands for:

C Cleanliness
H Hospitality
A Accuracy
M Maintenance (equipment and facilities)
P Product Quality
S Speed with Service

After discovering what the customers wanted, the company decided to make it an important part of their vision. At any Yum! restaurant you go to, the people will know about CHAMPS.

EMPOWERING FRONTLINE PEOPLE: THE KEY TO MAKING YOUR VISION COME ALIVE

Knowing about CHAMPS is one thing, but delivering excellence in each of these areas is another. That requires empowering your frontline people. Yum! is a poster child example of turning the traditional pyramid hierarchy upside down so that frontline associates closest to the customer are at the top. They know that only when that occurs will systematic Customer Mania be possible.

This empowerment philosophy is reflected everywhere at Yum!, particularly in people's titles. The person responsible for a cluster of five or six stores is not called a district manager but an area coach. Someone who is responsible for a region of three to four hundred restaurants is not a regional vice president, but a region coach. In between the region coach and the area coach is the market coach. Corporate is not called Corporate but the RSC—Restaurant Support Center. Language is a significant carrier of a culture; it imbeds an organization's values. For instance, certain isolated Pacific Island people have no word for stealing. At Yum! there is no word for "subordinate" and no room for "bosses." When it comes to creating Customer Mania, associates are responsible for making it happen, while the leadership plays a supportive, coaching, cheerleading role where they can be responsive to the associates' needs. That is key to empowering frontline folks.

A significant part of Customer Mania training now focuses on taking care of customer problems. If a waitperson or counter person has a customer with a problem, the team member is encouraged to solve it on the spot as opposed to talking to the manager. In fact, team members can create the way they take care of customers. They can do it their way. That makes it a little crazier, but that's the way Yum! likes it.

When I spoke at a KFC meeting a couple of years ago, I told the story of how Ritz-Carlton gives their frontline people a $2,000 discretionary fund to solve customer problems without checking with anyone. David Novak—who is a great learner—loved the idea of giving people discretionary funds. He later told us, "Our Customer Mania program now includes empowering team members to solve customer complaints right on the spot. They used to have to get the RGM to deal with problems. Now they can use up to $10 to respond to a customer issue.

"Some people in our organization said, 'Hey, if we let our team members do that, we'll end up going broke because we'll be giving all of our profits away.' And yet we've got the highest margin we've ever had in the company since we launched Customer Mania. So people aren't out there ripping us off. The half or one percent who were doing it before are probably still doing it. But this policy has had a big impact on team members. They feel respected and empowered; consequently our customers see us as much more responsive."

A $10 discretionary fund in a quick service restaurant is a lot of money. In Ritz-Carlton, which is a much higher–end operation, $2,000 is a lot of money. The point is, a discretionary fund becomes a competitive advantage when people closest to the customer feel they're in charge and can make decisions and solve problems.

GOING THE EXTRA MILE
FOR CUSTOMERS WITH A YES! ATTITUDE

Initially, when Pizza Hut—an organization that had always been run much more like American Airlines than Southwest Airlines—heard about a plan that empowered team members to give away free pizza or refund a customer's money without any particular checks or balances, they were horrified. But all that has changed.

David assigned his leaders to read the book *Built from Scratch*, about Home Depot. Ken Langone, who was a big player in the creation of Home Depot and who is on the Yum! board, was always talking about what a great culture they have at Home Depot. *Built from Scratch* has all these stories about how Home Depot people do incredible things for customers. Jerry Buss, COO of Pizza Hut, said, "You know what? I bet we've got just as many stories about people at Pizza Hut doing those things as Home Depot has—probably more, since we've been around longer and there are more Pizza Huts than there are Home Depots."

It was decided that every meeting would begin with someone sharing a Customer Mania story. Stories began to be collected about team members doing everything from pulling somebody out of an overturned truck and saving the day, to rescuing customers who'd locked their keys in the car, to just doing a great job taking care of customers. Soon a system was in place for sending out requests for great stories. So many stories came back that a Department of Recognition was needed. Christine Postolos, director of communications and recognition for Pizza Hut, collected all those inspiring stories into a book and gave them out to everyone. Two such collections have been distributed to date.

The sharing of stories generated a new kind of permission in the restaurants. The Customer Mania ethos says unless you're jeopardizing somebody's health or safety, whenever company policies and procedures conflict with what the customer wants, *"say yes to the customer."*

DUCKBUSTING:
OVERCOMING A BUREAUCRATIC MENTALITY

Something about bureaucratic environments seems to suck the life right out of people. As people pass through the portals to go to a bureaucratic workplace, it's as if their hearts shut down and their faces gray over. Yum! fights that trend with the power of positive energy.

Positive Energy
We execute with positive energy and intensity—
we hate bureaucracy and all the nonsense
that comes with it.

"Positive energy in our business is critical to creating Customer Maniacs," David Novak says, "so if you're one of those people who walk around with a dark cloud over them, you're on the wrong bus." Like so many companies, the biggest opportunity facing Yum! is building the competence and commitment of team members to overcome any bureaucratic mentality and become Customer Maniacs.

That the company's leaders are committed to the value of positive energy is clear. It runs like lightning throughout this organization. People at all levels are exuding positive energy—passion, excitement, team spirit, and a gung ho attitude. The payoff once again for the marshalling and cascading of all that positive energy is to have it happen for customers in the restaurants. That's what they mean when they say they want to put a Yum! on people's faces.

YUM!'S SCORECARD

Treating Its Customers the Right Way

6 out of 10

SEVERAL YEARS AGO on a golf trip to Ireland, our group went into an Irish pub where the staff had boomerangs on their shirts. When our waitress came over to take our order I asked, "Aren't boomerangs from Australia? Why are you all wearing them?"

She smiled and said, "When you throw a boomerang out, what does it do?"

I was quick to reply, "It comes back."

"That's exactly what we want you to do," she said with a twinkle in her eye.

When Customer Mania is alive and well, customers not only want to come back, they become part of your sales force. As raving fans, they want to brag about you. This is the passion for Yum!

At present, we would score Yum! a 6 on a 10-point scale. Customer Mania has cascaded throughout the management ranks, but except in a few isolated instances, they still haven't driven it through the roofs so that customers walking into any of their restaurants will be blown away with the service they get. This is the biggest challenge for the company going forward. Right now, they are halfway

(continued on facing page)

(continued from facing page)

there to their dream of creating a worldwide Customer Mania culture throughout all their restaurants. In fact, if you look at their own internal measures, only 53 percent of their restaurants are getting 100 percent CHAMPS scores, which means only half of the customers are getting all their expectations fulfilled. And as president and chief multibranding officer Aylwin Lewis says, "If we're missing even one letter of CHAMPS, we're letting our customers down and not delivering Customer Mania each and every transaction."

CHAPTER 5

STEP THREE
Treat Your People the Right Way

THE THIRD STEP IN BUILDING a company the right way is all about people. Everyone knows people are your most important resource. Yet most organizations do not have gung ho people—folks who are proud to work there.

BLANCHARD'S DREAM

LEADERSHIP THAT EMPHASIZES judgment, criticism, and evaluation is a relic of the past. Great leadership today is about treating people the right way by providing the support and encouragement they need to be their best. When you treat your people like winners, they treat your customers as if they're the most important people in the world. That's what creates raving fans and gets your cash register going ca-ching.

How do you create Customer Maniacs who will go the extra mile to create raving fans? You have to organize and integrate the four key human resource development functions:

1. Recruiting and hiring

2. Training and development

   3. Performance management

   4. Career development

In most organizations, different groups of people do each of these functions and they tend not to build on each other. In a world-class organization, however, not only are all these functions well integrated with the vision and direction, but the performance management function gets the most attention. Why?

When Spencer Johnson and I wrote *The One Minute Manager*, we had a saying:

People who feel good about themselves produce good results.

That's true. People who feel good about themselves work harder. But after that book came out I thought maybe I had gotten caught in the old human relations trap. You can't go around trying to make people feel good in a vacuum. So when I wrote *Putting the One Minute Manager to Work* with Bob Lorber, we changed that statement to read:

People who produce good results feel good about themselves.

The way to treat your people the right way and make them feel good about themselves is to help them win and accomplish their goals. That requires a good performance management system.

In the following sections we'll look at each of the four key human resource functions. When we get to performance management, there will be two additional sections: one on systems and processes and another on the development of a recognition culture. Without these two elements, the performance management system will never come alive.

GET THE RIGHT PEOPLE ON THE TEAM: RECRUITING AND HIRING

BLANCHARD'S DREAM

THE FIRST STEP in getting people to go the extra mile to create raving fans is recruiting and hiring the right people for your team. That involves looking for people with both competence and character. When we talk about competence, we're talking about whether they have the skills and experience to do the job you want them to do. If they don't, then what you are hiring are people with potential. With the proper training and development, you think they can learn to do that job well.

When it comes to character, what you're looking for are people who will be good citizens in your organization, people who will get excited about your vision and values. My wife Margie has said that leadership is love. "It's not about love; it *is* love—loving your vision and values, loving yourself, loving your customers, and loving your people." So when you're looking for people of character, you first want people who love what you do and what you stand for—your vision. In terms of loving yourself, you want people who love themselves with humility. In other words, they're self-confident, but they're not people who think that they're the center of the universe. They are more interested in serving others than being served. When it comes to loving your customers and your people, we're talking about hiring people who love other human beings. They're the kind of people you want because they'll be great teammates. They're excited about dealing with your customers, suppliers, and other people who interact with your organization.

If you have to choose between hiring people with competence or character, my experience is, hire for character first, and train for competence. Every time we have made a mistake—hired the wrong person—in retrospect we realized that person lacked love or passion in two or more of those areas. It's hard, if not impossible, to train people for character. We do know, though, you've got to get the right people on your team so that they can align not only with the results you want, but also with the way you want people to behave.

YUM!'S REALITY: RECRUITING AND HIRING

MOST COMPANIES LEAVE selection pretty much to chance. They say, "Get good people," but they don't have a process in place for that. Many of them have not clearly defined what they're looking for in the first place. When it comes to hiring, Yum! is anything but *laissez faire.* Dan Adams, vice president of human resources at Yum! Restaurants International, says, "In my view, of all the drivers to build capability, selection is the single most important one."

THE DESIRE FOR A VALUES MATCH

Gregg Dedrick told us, "When we formed Tricon we had a lot of corporate jobs to fill up and we didn't have a corporate office. Our strategy was to be very open and vulnerable with people about our values. We said, 'This is what our culture is; if this excites you, let's talk. But hey, if this isn't you, if you think it's hokey or stupid or not your cup of tea, don't come here because you're not going to be happy and you're not going to do well.'

"On the proactive side, David started commissioning some searches for people who modeled what we wanted, people who were passionate about the restaurant business, who really had a reputation for our kind of values and could really help us bring it to the next level. Jonathan Blum, our public affairs guy, started to get some articles published and the word got out about us.

"Even in those early messages we were communicating our values base. We got some press in the trade journals and that helped create that pull for people. People would call up and say, 'Hey, my adrenaline was rushing when I read this article. I'd love to come talk with you guys.' Jonathan really did a good job getting our positioning out there when we were a young company. We didn't want to be bragging—we didn't have the results yet to brag—we just wanted to set the stage by telling who we were and what we were trying to do. We were saying, 'We have a unique story and we want people and investors who believe in it.' "

GETTING THE RIGHT PEOPLE
AT THE RESTAURANT LEVEL

Roger Karolick, Pizza Hut franchisee, describes how he's been adopting an innovative idea to get the right people at the restaurant level:

"The way most of our industry works, most people figure that, hey, you got over 200 percent turnover so you take the first thing that comes through the door. You think you don't have the time to really qualify people, so if an applicant's got two arms, two legs, and a heartbeat, they're hired. You drop them in the job and hope they work out okay. Most of them disappear within the first ninety days, so you're spinning all the time.

"Yum! introduced what they call the realistic job preview. Before you give the final hiring decision to an individual you bring them back, take them through the restaurant, talk to them a little bit, let them observe what's going on in your restaurant's environment. Try to observe them as they observe what's going on, and get a feel for whether they like what they see; ask them questions about that. This is just one more way of trying to get inside the person and determine whether he or she is going to be a good fit on my team. The realistic job preview has had a real impact on our turnover.

"Along with having candidates complete an application, we have what we call a team member readiness inventory (TMRI), an instrument that Pizza Hut developed to screen for the kind of person who works best in the hospitality industry. At our annual restaurant general manager meetings we have a forum that brings together our best managers. We pick a subject and they talk about how they are achieving great results in that particular area. Recently we had one on turnover, and one of the questions was, 'How do you go about hiring people?' Every one of them was following the team members selection process using the TMRI. Those are the guys that have very low turnover, and to a person, they said they'd been using the realistic job preview."

RIGOROUS HIRING

Amanda Huntley, a Pizza Hut RGM from the United Kingdom, points to a direct payoff from her rigorous attention to hiring the right people—low turnover. "Previously it was a case of, advertise and the first twenty who came in got a job. That's not the way I do it now. My turnover is at 40 percent and I want to keep it there. I want people who are enthusiastic, and it all comes out on what I call the interview stage. I wouldn't say they have to do an audition, but they have to come across with spirit and charisma.

"We do role plays in interviews to have them show how they would behave in certain situations. You can get a lot of information when you put people in scenarios like that. We also ask candidates how they would behave under pressure or in the midst of challenges. Would they just do the basics—what's required (which is not the type of people I want in my business) or would they go beyond what was expected of them from the customer's point of view?

"We also use the TMRI. Once we've had them on the interview stage and they've gone through the TMRI, we put them through a little on-the-job experience. We put them into a uniform, put them in the environment, and let them shadow a team member for a few hours. That way we can see how they react, how they work with the team. Will they fit into the team? How will they interact with customers? How much initiative will they show?" Huntley enthusiastically concludes, "The more rigorous I get, the better candidates I get. Good people love to be tested."

GETTING THE WRONG PEOPLE OFF THE TEAM

David Novak does not wait around for the Yum! culture to create itself. He believes that a leader coming into a new position can produce an immediate change for the better by finding people who shouldn't be on the bus—people who aren't supportive of the vision and direction—and replacing them.

"When I go into companies," David says, "I go hunting. I look for the easy pickings, the people that need to go. Early on I'd had my doubts about one company executive. I thought his values were not in sync with the culture.

"One day our recognition band—a group of talented folks who go around with kazoos and other instruments, singing and putting on a show to celebrate people and cheer them on—came near his office. He got all upset, complaining he had work to do and this noise was a distraction. I told him, 'If you don't like watching an assistant get recognized and seeing tears in her eyes, if you think that's stupid and phony, you need to go somewhere else.' The man soon found himself working somewhere else."

Chief financial officer Dave Deno is more the prototypical Yum! leader. He believes in driving the business the right way, with a collaborative rather than command-and-control style. Being CFO requires that Dave make most final calls, but the way he brings people with him makes them feel better about being on his bus.

Getting the wrong people off the team is handled with care at Yum! "When people wanted to leave the company," Dedrick told us, "I actually encouraged them to let us know and work with us, so we could help them find the right next place in or outside of Yum! We try to be humane and to communicate that we care about you as a person. That gets a lot of play for us. People see that we're different, that we work with them—whether or not they're leaving on their own terms. Ultimately, people will judge your culture by how well you treat people who are in a powerless situation."

THE ATTRACTION OF A CUSTOMER MANIA CULTURE

Not everyone who gets off the team stays off the team. Roger Eaton, who joined the company as a finance director for KFC Australia in 1990, left to pursue an exciting opportunity to become CEO of a cinema company in the United States.

"Within a couple of months of leaving, I knew I'd lost something," he says. "I kept talking about this fantastic organization I'd left."

Five years later the managing director position in Yum!'s South Pacific division opened up and Roger "was back in a flash. The Customer Mania culture is so attractive. We have so much fun here. It's the people end of this business that makes it so special. What got me back so quickly was that the PepsiCo high-performance culture still existed. It was very apparent, however, that the passion for operating restaurants and the incredible people who run them were now the primary drivers of the Yum! culture. This was quite different from the PepsiCo days when that culture was found pocketed in only some of the restaurant operations and was clearly foreign to the beverage and snack food divisions."

He also talks about how deeply he appreciates Yum!'s alignment around a positive purpose. "I'm ridiculously passionate about this company," he says with a laugh.

YUMI'S SCORECARD

Recruiting and Hiring

7 out of 10

IN TERMS OF GETTING THE RIGHT PEOPLE on the team, we would rate Yum! a 7. They have a strategy in place to make sure they are getting the right people. In the last six years, the company has done a better job of selection and RGM turnover has gone from 28 percent in 2000 to 17 percent in 2003; the industry average is 33 percent. Team member turnover has gone from 181 percent in 2000 to 114 percent in 2003; the industry average is 136 percent. Even though Yum! is leading the industry, given the fact that turnover is still very high, they have to do even better.

Retention is a never-ending task. If you don't pump people up during the hiring process and get them excited about being a part of your organization, the swinging door will continue to hit you as former employees head down the street to another enterprise. We know this is a top-of-mind issue for the company's leadership team, which has established a bold goal of 50 percent team member turnover. Our experience says that most of their competitors are not at their level of sophistication in hiring and recruiting. The better the hiring and retention, the better the results.

GIVE PEOPLE THE RIGHT START: TRAINING AND DEVELOPMENT

BLANCHARD'S DREAM

ONCE YOU HAVE PEOPLE ABOARD, you have to give them the appropriate training and development. Obviously, they have to learn the skills and competencies necessary to do their jobs well. The more prior experience people have for a particular job, the less competency training they'll need. But you have to remember that jobs are changing all the time and one of the hallmarks of great organizations is that they are committed to constantly retraining and educating their people so they have cutting-edge knowledge in their work.

As I mentioned earlier, it's hard to train people in character, so the real issue is, how do you discover—once you've made a judgment about people's character—whether you've got the right people on the team? One important vehicle is your orientation program. And yet many organizations don't have an orientation program. People report to work the first day and they're on the job. Their orientation is hit or miss.

At Disney theme parks no one starts work until going through the two-day Traditions Program. During those two days they learn about the legacy of Walt Disney and the four operational values and how those values are expected to impact their behavior in each of their jobs. A number of people who go through the Disney Traditions orientation never get to work at Disney. And it's not just Disney's choice. Some of the people decide they don't want to work there. You have to find some way to get your vision—purpose, picture of the future, values, and key goals—into the mind of every new employee before they even start.

Let's say you know you have the right people on your team character-wise. You have given them the appropriate competency training to do their job. Now you are ready for them to perform—to be a contributor to your organization.

YUM!'S REALITY: TRAINING AND DEVELOPMENT

HOW WELL DOES YUM! DO in giving people the tools necessary to perform on the job? The company has extensive formal training programs to spread the word on values and give restaurant operators around the world the know-how they need to run great restaurants.

IDENTIFYING AND TEACHING BEST PRACTICES

Everyone loves to be part of an organization that is innovative and creative. I have never seen a group of top managers as open to learning and benchmarking the innovations of others as Yum! They learn from others' successes and give credit to the source. When it comes to innovation, they are not stupid. They realize that all bright ideas do not originate with them. You name an innovation, and they'll try it. That's exciting to smart businesspeople.

It was in studying and following the lead of best-practice organizations such as Wal-Mart, Home Depot, Southwest Airlines, and General Electric that David Novak and his cofounders laid the foundation for what was to become Yum! Brands. Benchmarking is how they got their systems, visiting the best and constructing an integrated set of systems. Many companies that are the largest in their industry are characterized by an attitude of, "You can learn from me." Yum! reverses this. It's ever on the hunt for how to make its operation better by learning from others.

Gregg Dedrick comments on Yum!'s senior leadership training program, called *Taking People with You*. "We don't re-create the wheel," he says, "we find out what works and apply it to the business. The principle is, 'Don't be too proud to learn and change.' We use the 'We Learn from Anyone' principle of executive training. The first thing we teach is to get rid of the NIH (not-invented-here) mentality and get rid of bureaucracy. In our 33,000 restaurants we have huge opportunities for people to make things happen. We try to learn from them and transfer knowledge, so everybody can learn and use best practices. When you model the behavior of taking best practices from anywhere, it encourages continuous learning. We constantly cite who we learned from so people understand what it takes to be excellent."

It's clear to us that Yum! wants the best practices they can build or preferably find. Why put a lot of time into something when you can get it better somewhere else and implement change so much faster? The Learning No. 1 slide from the *Taking People with You* leadership program that David Novak facilitates is a good summary of some of the best practices we have found.

TRAINING FUELS THE
CUSTOMER MANIA STRATEGY

The *Taking People with You* and *Building the Yum! Dynasty* programs are for the top company leaders and the franchise owners and their key associates—about six hundred people. David personally teaches both of these three-day programs four or five times a year. *Taking People with You* is about how to build and align your team around a

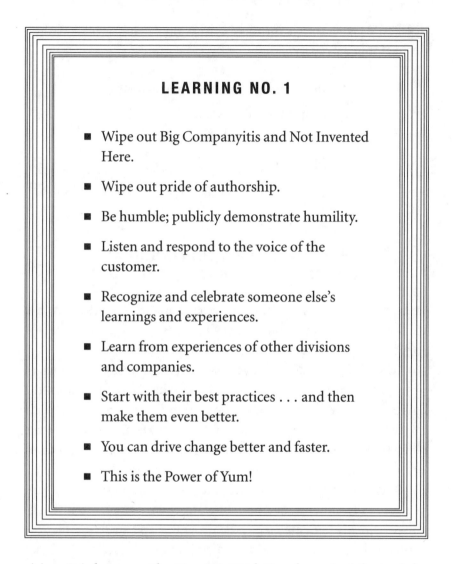

LEARNING NO. 1

- Wipe out Big Companyitis and Not Invented Here.

- Wipe out pride of authorship.

- Be humble; publicly demonstrate humility.

- Listen and respond to the voice of the customer.

- Recognize and celebrate someone else's learnings and experiences.

- Learn from experiences of other divisions and companies.

- Start with their best practices . . . and then make them even better.

- You can drive change better and faster.

- This is the Power of Yum!

vision. It is heavy on the *How We Work Together* principles and the role of the leader.

Building the Yum! Dynasty is in essence a statement of what it takes to build a great company. David and the founders benchmarked fifteen top companies that deliver sustainable positive results and talked with experts who have studied or done it. They distilled their learnings into five drivers they believe will fuel their do-over into a dynasty:

1. A culture where everybody makes a difference.
2. Customer and sales mania.
3. Competitive brand differentiation.
4. Continuity in people and process.
5. Consistency in results by beating year-ago measures in every area.

THE IMPACT OF TRAINING SOARS WHEN TOP MANAGERS ARE INVOLVED

Francisco Rovira, a franchisee in El Salvador who owns thirty-five Pizza Hut restaurants, told us how his sense of isolation from the corporation was reversed when Yum! began to be formed.

"David Novak wants to have a one-system philosophy. As a result of his efforts we've come to understand what is happening in the company and we've become committed to the vision and the *How We Work Together* principles. Up to the point David started this, we had pretty much been on our own when it came to culture and strategy. We've only started to understand our own company since then."

Rovira found that the culture David was instilling was very supportive of the things he and his fellow storeowners believed in. Franchisees directly benefited from the programs and structure that the company leaders shared. He tells of attending a leadership seminar taught by David:

"It truly was a life-changing experience for me. I couldn't believe that this man, with all the responsibilities he had, would have time to spend three days in a room with all of us. I remember the price of the company's stock was falling—that particular week it had dropped significantly—but he just stayed there, going to dinner with us and taking the time to talk with each of us. I admired that very much. It motivated me to take all the information, structure, strategy, and the *How We Work Together* principles and cascade it into our organization."

David Novak continues to invest a significant portion of his time in presenting four or five leadership development seminars a year around the world, whether in Louisville, Hong Kong, London, Mexico City, or Kuwait City. This leader-led approach is standard procedure in all training at all levels of the organization. The message is this: If the CEO can take three days out of his schedule four or five times a year, then other company leaders can take the time to train their people.

The positive results have been significant. "From our perspective here in our small country of El Salvador it's hard to know what's happening," says Rovira, "but if it works for the rest of the organization the way it has worked for us, he is certainly making an impact."

Rovira's response was not an unusual one from the franchise owners we talked to in the United States and abroad. These leadership programs, coupled with the cascading of values, are a powerful way to communicate the company vision and spread its customer-focused, people-first, performance-based culture.

There are additional benefits. The chief people officer and other key leaders usually appear during the three-day training program. The company people get to know franchisees, understand their issues, and build relationships with them. The fact that the program is based on best practices compels owners to take the learning and get it into their operations. Getting the franchisee system on the bus is a continuing passion at Yum!

DEVELOPING CHAMPIONS THROUGH TRAINING

Extensive training for all levels in the restaurant and for area coaches builds and strengthens the Customer Mania mindset. The Developing Champions program uses a combination of on-the-job coaching and classroom time to teach both leadership skills and the nitty-gritty details of running a restaurant. High Impact Coaching, another leader-led program that has been cascaded throughout the operations organization, builds capability and drives a coaching mentality.

Yum! University was created as a way to teach and institutionalize the Dynasty Model. For example, the week-long Operations College teaches company and franchise operators everything they ever wanted to know about how to run a great restaurant. It covers leadership, restaurant details, and people development as well as all of the company's best practice restaurant systems and processes. Ops College is yet another system that rigorously maintains Yum!'s people/performance equilibrium.

The company has built similar programs in marketing, finance, human resources, development, and other areas. It uses these colleges to drive functional excellence, leadership, and its Customer Mania culture around the world.

TRAINING THE FRONTLINE PEOPLE
FOR A BETTER LIFE

There is a growing movement in the company not only to train the frontline people in the basic skills they need to do the jobs they've been hired for, but also to teach them life skills that will make them successful in whatever they decide to do. Skills like how to listen to the voice of the customer, be empathetic to customer needs, exceed expectations within reason, and recover when they make a mistake. The company encourages its team members to solve customer issues on the spot without turning to their restaurant managers. They believe that by staying after this day after day, year after year, they will become the very best in their business at providing consistently good service.

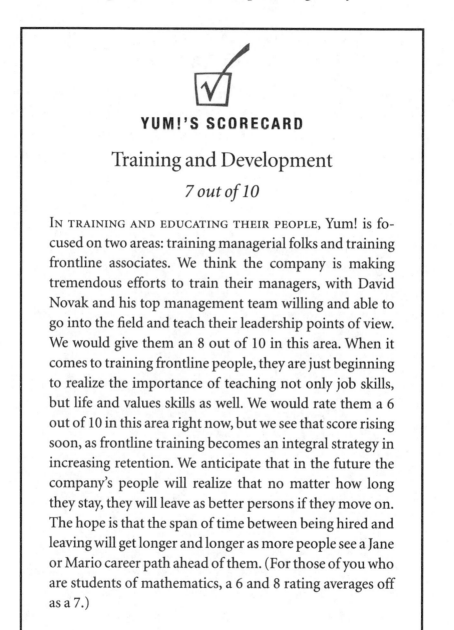

YUM!'S SCORECARD

Training and Development

7 out of 10

IN TRAINING AND EDUCATING THEIR PEOPLE, Yum! is focused on two areas: training managerial folks and training frontline associates. We think the company is making tremendous efforts to train their managers, with David Novak and his top management team willing and able to go into the field and teach their leadership points of view. We would give them an 8 out of 10 in this area. When it comes to training frontline people, they are just beginning to realize the importance of teaching not only job skills, but life and values skills as well. We would rate them a 6 out of 10 in this area right now, but we see that score rising soon, as frontline training becomes an integral strategy in increasing retention. We anticipate that in the future the company's people will realize that no matter how long they stay, they will leave as better persons if they move on. The hope is that the span of time between being hired and leaving will get longer and longer as more people see a Jane or Mario career path ahead of them. (For those of you who are students of mathematics, a 6 and 8 rating averages off as a 7.)

GIVE PEOPLE THE RIGHT HELP:
PERFORMANCE MANAGEMENT

ONCE THE RIGHT PEOPLE are on the team and properly trained, performance management is the key vehicle that keeps their eyes on the target and helps them achieve their goals. To get people to go the extra mile and become Customer Maniacs, you must know the right way to manage their performance.

BLANCHARD'S DREAM

YOU HAVE THREE CHOICES when you hire people. One, you can hire a winner, somebody who already has experience in what you're asking them to do. What you need to do with them is be clear on their goals and objectives, and then let them run with the ball. The second choice you have is to hire a potential winner. That is somebody who, with appropriate training and coaching, you think you can develop into a high performer. The third choice is prayer. Unfortunately a lot of organizations hire people, then give them some haphazard training and pray that the person hired will become a winner. Great organizations don't leave that to chance. They have a well-oiled performance management system.

There are three parts to managing people's performance. The first is *performance planning.* After everyone is clear on the vision and direction, it's during performance planning that you agree upon the goals and objectives and what you're trying to accomplish. During performance planning, it's okay for the traditional hierarchy to be alive and well, because if there's a disagreement between a manager and a direct report about goals, who wins? The manager, because that person represents the goals and objectives of the total organization.

The second aspect of performance management is *performance monitoring and feedback*. Feedback is the breakfast of champions. This is where you invert the pyramid and turn the hierarchy upside down on a day-to-day basis. Now the manager is doing everything he or she can do to help team members be successful. This is where servant leadership kicks in. Now the manager works for his or her people, praising their progress and redirecting inappropriate performance.

The third and final aspect of performance management is *performance evaluation*. This is where a manager and direct report sit down and assess the performance of the team member over time.

Which of these three—performance planning, performance monitoring and feedback, or performance evaluation—do most organizations devote the greatest amount of time to? It's performance evaluation. I go into organization after organization and people say to me, "You're going to love our new performance evaluation form." I always laugh, because I think most of them can be thrown out. Why? Because these forms measure things that nobody knows how to evaluate. For example, initiative or willingness to take responsibility. Or promotability—that's a good one. When no one knows how to win on evaluation, they focus most of their energy up the hierarchy. After all, if you have a good relationship with your boss, you have a higher probability of getting a good evaluation.

Some organizations do a good job on performance planning and set very clear goals. However, after goal setting, what do you think happens to those goals? Most often, they get filed and no one looks at them until they are told, "It's time for performance evaluation." Now everybody's running around bumping into each other trying to find the goals.

Of the three aspects of performance management, which is the one where the least time is spent? That's the day-to-day observing and monitoring of performance. This is where performance coaching really comes alive. It's where feedback—praising progress and redirecting inappropriate behavior—moves to center stage. It is the most important aspect of managing people's performance.

To illustrate my thinking in this area, let me share my ten-year experience as a college professor. I was always in trouble. I was investigated by some of the best faculty committees. What drove the faculty crazy more than anything was that at the beginning of every class I gave students the final exam. When the faculty found out about that, they asked, "What are you doing?"

Not knowing why they were questioning me, I said, "I'm confused."

They said, "You act it."

I said, "I thought we were supposed to teach these students."

They said, "You are, but don't give the students the final exam ahead of time!"

I said, "Not only am I going to give them the final exam ahead of time, what do you think I'm going to do throughout the semester? I'm going to teach them the answers, so that when they get to the final exam, they get As. You see life is all about getting As, not some stupid normal distribution curve."

How many of you go out and hire losers? Do you go around saying, "We lost some of our best losers last year, so let's go out and hire some new ones to fill those low spots"? No, you go out and hire either winners—people who are already experienced in doing what you want them to do—or potential win-ners—people you think can become winners if you train and coach them.

Giving people the final exam ahead of time is equivalent to performance planning. Now they know exactly what's expected of them. Teaching people the answers is observing and monitoring performance and providing feedback on progress. If you see somebody doing something right, you give them an "atta boy" or "atta girl." If they do something wrong, you don't beat them up. Instead you say, "Wrong answer. What do you think would be the right answer?" In other words, you redirect them. And finally, giving people the same exam you gave them at the beginning of the semester is performance evaluation. There should be no surprises in performance evaluation. Everyone should know what the test is going to be, and then get the help throughout the year to achieve a high score on it. When you have a forced distribution where a certain percentage of your people have to lose, you lose everyone's trust. All they are concerned about is looking after number one. If you help people get As, then you have a performance management system that will ignite them to blow your customers away.

YUM!'S REALITY: PERFORMANCE COACHING

PERFORMANCE MANAGEMENT is important at Yum!, yet they're very careful about using the word *management* because they feel it often smacks of bureaucracy. What they didn't want was a performance management system that involved filling out endless forms and carrying out top-down orders. So, as they always seem to do, they gave performance management a complete do-over, with coaching at its center.

Coaching and Support
We coach and support each other.

COACHING THE YUM! WAY

A coach's job is to help stars shine and help teams win. A coach is someone who's nearby; not some suit in a distant city. Good coaches have to be more than figureheads; they have to know the rules of the game and how it's played. And coaches can't be successful unless their teams are successful. In the eyes of Yum! leadership, coaching is an ideal way to create and spread the new culture.

Of all the innovations we discussed with Yum! folks, the thing they wanted to talk about most was coaching, and the power of it. The company's performance coaching system is designed to align performance with values; this provides a basis for personal development. Listen to their voices to see how central coaching is to driving their Customer Mania culture.

Blue Chip Goal Setting. The leadership at Yum! realizes that all good performance starts with clear goals. As a result, their goal setting system is well organized. Here's how it works:

People set goals at the beginning of each year; the most important goals are called blue chips. The focus of blue chips is on results. Key goals are set from the top and cascaded and supported all the way down to the restaurants. Members sit down with their coaches, identify their most important goals, and make sure there is a clear line of sight between the goals set at the top of the organization and theirs. The coaching process is designed to work on an ongoing basis to help people achieve their blue chips.

The midyear evaluation is based on 360-degree feedback from people all around an associate; 80 percent of the review concentrates on personal and career development, 20 percent on blue chips. The focus is on personal development—the how of getting results, the extent to which the person walks the talk on values and acts like the leader.

Half of this feedback deals with the *How We Work Together* principles, the other half with the *How We Lead* leadership responsibilities. Discussion centers on review of the 360-degree feedback and identifying opportunities. It also includes career development discussions.

At the end of the year leaders meet with their managers for Performance Achievement Discussions. Now the emphasis changes. Eighty percent of the focus is on results, 20 percent on the how.

The Task of a Coach. Tim Morrison, Taco Bell's head coach for the Central Region, describes the task of a coach: "I view my responsibilities as helping to create an environment where people feel good about where they work and what they do. Part of that is to know they're valued, to know they have an opportunity to do whatever they want in this organization. Maybe that means being the best cook you can possibly be, or maybe it means being a cook today and having David Novak's job in ten years.

"I'm responsible for creating an environment where people get the proper training, feedback, development, and recognition. If I do that, everything else takes care of itself. In my mind, the *How We Work Together* principles are a perfect construct to do that."

Coach First and Coach Again. Coaching takes time. Even David admits that on occasion his impatience has caused him to forget his rule of "coach first and coach again."

"We had a CFO at KFC when I first came here who really drove me nuts. KFC hadn't grown the business for years. At every meeting I was in with him, all he talked about was ripping out costs, reducing the quality of our ingredients, and saving pennies here and pennies there. So when Wayne Calloway, chairman of PepsiCo at the time, came to town I said, 'Hey Wayne, this guy has to go.'

"Wayne says, 'I'm surprised; he's one of the smartest guys we have in the company. Have you told him how you feel about him?'

'Well, no not yet, but I know he's got to go.'

"He said, 'Why don't you go tell him what your problems are, and see how he does?' I mean I had this guy in my sights—he was gone.

"So I went to him and I said, 'I'm here to grow a business. When you want to cut costs, come talk to me privately, and we will deal with those issues. When you come to work I want you to help me grow the business. From now on I want you to look in the mirror every day, and see *Mr. Growth* stamped on your forehead, and that's all I want you to talk about in the meetings. All you're going to focus on publicly is *grow the business.*'

"Well, he took that feedback, because he wanted to be successful. He went out and met with RGMs and learned how much they love recognition. After that, he started spending more money on recognition. In the process he helped us grow and became one of the biggest proponents of our culture. It was a coaching issue. I learned: coach first, coach again. You gotta help them first, and then do it again. If nothing happens, they're probably on the wrong bus."

Coaching Is Helping—Not a Walk Outside. Pizza Hut regional coach Roman Saenz describes his first encounter with the positive power of coaching:

"It was my first experience with Aylwin Lewis, who was COO at Pizza Hut at that time, soon after David Novak took over. I had just been promoted to area coach. When I took over the area, I had to let about five managers go in my first six months. We were really focusing on promoting people from within and based on my past experience I moved some people up. People who really worked hard and had a lot of integrity. So they were still green. Very, very green.

"I had just promoted an RGM at one of my stores. Aylwin Lewis walks into the store with his entourage, totally unannounced. It blindsided everyone. We had no idea he was coming. When I walked in he'd already been there for about thirty minutes. I was scared. First thing I'm thinking, I just got promoted, I'm about to get canned. My experience with unannounced visits prior to Yum! didn't have me looking forward to a positive experience. Instead he looked at me and said, 'How can I help? What is it that you need to get your area straightened out?'

"I said, 'Hey, I've got four units without RGMs, others who have new RGMs. This RGM has just been here two weeks, this is his second week, so he's like scared to death.'

"He goes, 'How can I support you?'

"I told him, 'Well right now I'm just having a hard time being at all those stores.' At that time I had fifteen stores, four had new people, four without anybody, and for me to be able to support them was very difficult.

"He said, 'Tell you what, I'll give you a call Monday'—this was on Friday—'and we'll get you some help for the next four weekends, so you can be there and help develop your new RGMs, let them get their feet wet and settle in. I'll call first thing Monday morning.'

"Aylwin got maybe twenty people to help me over the next four weekends. He had Restaurant Support Center (RSC) staff working with us on weekends to help us. These people worked at the RSC during the week and with us on the weekends. They were experienced people. At that time there was this message from the RSC— "Backing the Front"—referring to the restaurants as our frontline. It was a big marching cry: 'We're going back in the field, making sure our restaurants are getting what they need.' We used to get that kinda stuff under the old management all the time. But what Aylwin said is what he did.

"Before that I probably would have been pulled outside, and told everything I was doing wrong. You're already in the weeds, feeling bad about what's going on, and you're trying to fix it, and that was what happened. A walk outside."

Anybody Can Coach Anybody. Coaching is not limited to leader-associate relationships at Yum! One of the field leaders we talked to at KFC said, "You coach up, sideways, and down." He recalled a time when he was working at Pizza Hut and Aylwin Lewis was chief operating officer:

"Aylwin is one of the best leaders I have ever seen—one of my key role models—and a driver of our culture around the world. But everybody has a bad day now and then. Maybe two. We had a region of about fifty restaurants in Columbus that were in terrible shape; twelve that didn't even have an RGM. So we brought an RGM up from Florida to take over a delivery restaurant. This guy does a great job, doubles weekly revenue within a few of months.

"Aylwin and I go down for a visit. Aylwin walks into the restaurant, looks around, then gives the RGM a lecture on training his employees to clean better. The guy was devastated. When we got outside the restaurant, I told Aylwin what I felt had happened and the negative impact I thought his behavior had on the RGM. We talked about it for a while and he thanked me. It takes a great relationship with your boss to have this kind of conversation, and if he has a big ego, it doesn't happen.

"In another situation, Aylwin totally rounded down on me three times in a row. He hit on me for three things I'd said I would do, without giving me a chance to explain what was going on. At Yum! we always want to round *up* on people—that is, don't make assumptions about their intentions. One of our values is 'Belief in people, trust in positive intentions.' So it sounded to me like he thought I was goofing off or something. This bothered me, so after a couple of days I went and talked to him. He said, 'You're right, I'm sorry.'

"We hold each other accountable. Being the president or CEO or anybody doesn't mean you're not accountable. It's really great to have the kind of culture and relationships where you can have these kinds of conversations. You don't have to spend a lot of energy worrying about your relationship with your boss or being the victim. By telling these stories we make ourselves available and people feel comfortable in holding us accountable, because we don't have to be perfect."

Coaching Can Challenge. Coaching doesn't always mean merely listening and trying to "lead the witness." Sometimes it involves confrontation and conflict. One of David Novak's direct reports reiterates the notion that coaching goes both ways:

"One of the things I love about this culture is the use of the word *coach*—and the fact that anybody can coach anybody. I experienced one of those moments when I had a major public disagreement with David Novak in my first six months at the company. We're very strong people, and we got into it in a meeting with his team and my team. And neither of one of us was happy about it.

"We stewed about it for a couple of days and then decided to talk about it. David took the lead in coaching, which was good because I was still very angry. He used an exercise that we were taught at KFC—an exercise called the Accountability Ladder. It's a process that helps you take responsibility for your own behavior. You know how people go around playing the victim game, telling everybody how badly they were treated? In the exercise you get to identify a time when you played the victim, only this time you tell the same person the story a few times. It's amazing how quickly the energy drains out of you when you play the victim. Energy is only sustained if you keep telling different people. I didn't know about any of this when David and I met to discuss the meeting.

"So David said, 'Tell your victim's story, I want to hear it.' And I said, 'What's a victim story? I hate the word; never been one and never going to be one!'

David said, 'Tell me your story about how you were treated and how you felt about it—what an idiot I was, what drove you crazy. Be the victim and just tell it as long as you need to.' And I thought, 'That's interesting. Nobody's ever asked me for my whole story before.' So I played along, saying, 'I have never had anybody be so condescending, and you did it in front of my people. It was disrespectful and humiliating.' I really got into it and did a full data dump. Then David did the same thing right back—a total whine.

"Finally David said, 'Now this time let's be accountable for the outcome. What could you and I have done differently to change the outcome?' And boy, did he make me think. There were a number of things I could've done instead of participating in and escalating the conflict. He really forced me to go back through my experience of the meeting. Then he took responsibility and did the same thing, and we compared notes. In twenty-four years, I have never had a coaching session that taught me as much.

"To do that kind of coaching you have to be pretty comfortable with who you are. You have to get your ego out of the way. David could have just relived the event from his point of view. So often that's exactly what happens. Instead he said, 'Let's go forward—this is behind us.'"

Coaching is about helping people identify problems and develop solutions. At this company, anyone can get coaching from anyone.

A DAY IN THE LIFE OF A COACH

Chuck Boone, area coach for Taco Bell, summarized a lot of what we saw as we shadowed the company's area coaches:

"Let me tell you what a day in the life of an area coach is like. There's lots of interaction with the restaurant. In the morning you get the numbers. You get a voice message from the team members who closed the night before. If there's some good performance— real consistent good performance—you want to call the units real quick. One or two minute conversations like: 'Hey, great job, keep the focus up today.'

"If there's some problem, you definitely want to spend a little bit more time calling them and asking questions. 'Did you recount the inventory?' Just take them through a couple steps that they get the hang of real quick and they're almost ready for your call the next morning. Probably that's about an hour of your time in the morning, just capturing the results and going back and making those phone calls to reinforce or to go ahead and give them some coaching to improve that day. That gets the morning started.

"Then I usually have two four-hour, in-depth coaching sessions at two restaurants. I spend a good deal of that time with the RGM. If they're out of the store for whatever reason, I have it with the senior assistant or assistant manager.

"Typically, you go to the restaurant and you walk around and say hi to everybody, make sure you wish everybody a good day. If there are customers, I would greet them and ask them how their visit is going and if there is anything we could do to make it better. You go and meet with the RGM and for twenty minutes you run down what's going on lately, or ask them, How's it going? Then you dig in and take a look at the restaurant. It's a very structured piece of that four hours. We both have detailed reports on all major aspects of the functioning of the store. They're used to it. It's something they're anticipating. Some of them have gotten so used to it; they're ahead of the game.

"Probably the best part of the day is sitting down with the RGM in the dining room and having a really good conversation. For two hours I can go deep, either on something I see they need help with or something they bring up. Our high impact coaching model is called the EARS model. EARS stands for Explore, Analyze, Respond, and make it Stick. Through asking different questions you get to the core problem of what they're struggling with. You're not going to tell them what's wrong. They get to see it themselves. They come up with it. It's almost like they have an epiphany about the real issue. You just helped them get to that point.

"After you help them work out a way to handle the opportunity, the next time you're in the store you make sure that you check in with them on that issue to make sure it's taken care of. If they've made progress, it provides me with the opportunity to recognize them."

The guidelines from Chuck Boone's account of a day in the life of a coach suggest that self-discovery is the basis of it all—you want the person to own the learning, to be self-accountable, and self-watchful as a result of the interaction. It's an intensely personal process: two people working toward the same end, one who is acting not as a boss, but as a facilitator of the other's chance to improve performance.

The coaches in this company teach without telling. They support discovery of answers by leading people to them. Rob Savage, chief operating officer of Taco Bell, says, "Of course, in the short term it's a lot quicker to just tell them. But coaching is not an option here. It is the process through which we live and drive our values."

CAN COACHING BE TAUGHT?

The company leaders think coaching can be taught, but only if the coach doesn't act like a know-it-all. "All you need is one person to get vulnerable," says Aylwin Lewis. "The minute a leader shares something they did wrong or that they wish they could have done over, the walls really break down and you have this tremendous connection around how to drive performance." Big egos don't work long at Yum! because they just don't fit in.

David Novak makes no bones about it—he believes coaching can be taught and thinks that the company's performance coaching operation is the best in the world. Because it has the systems, processes, and recognition culture to support its coaching program, we think the company has the potential to be world-class, too.

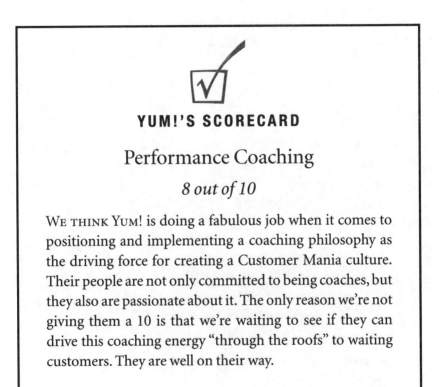

YUM!'S SCORECARD

Performance Coaching

8 out of 10

WE THINK YUM! is doing a fabulous job when it comes to positioning and implementing a coaching philosophy as the driving force for creating a Customer Mania culture. Their people are not only committed to being coaches, but they also are passionate about it. The only reason we're not giving them a 10 is that we're waiting to see if they can drive this coaching energy "through the roofs" to waiting customers. They are well on their way.

GET PEOPLE WIRED IN: DEVELOPING THE RIGHT SYSTEMS AND PROCESSES

BLANCHARD'S DREAM

IF YOU WANT TO CREATE raving fans and Customer Maniacs so your cash register goes ca-ching, you can't leave it up to chance. "The road to hell is paved with good intentions." It's an old but true saying. My experience suggests that nothing good ever happens by accident. For example, I'm sure you know somebody who is very thoughtful. They seem to always remember your birthday. How do they do that? They have a system in their organizer or Palm Pilot so that, a week to ten days before your birthday, up pops information that ignites their good intention to remember your birthday. Effective leadership is like that. It is more a discipline than an art. It requires good systems. In the last section, we talked about performance management and how vital that is to making sure that your people produce good results and in the process can feel good about themselves. What makes a performance management system effective?

In working with Bob Lorber on *Putting the One Minute Manager to Work,* we identified five systems that must be in place if an organization is to have an effective performance management system: accountability, data/information, feedback, training, and recognition. In other words, for people to perform at a high level, they need to know what they are being asked to do (accountability) and what good behavior looks like (data/information). Then they need to know how well they are doing (feedback). If their performance is lacking, they need redirection (training). If their performance is positive, they need to be caught doing something right and praised (recognition).

SYSTEM NO. 1: ACCOUNTABILITY

For an organization's goals to be reached, every person—whether working individually or in a group—needs to know what he or she will be held accountable for. All good performance starts with clear goals. That's why One Minute Goal Setting is the first secret of the One Minute Manager. The clearer you make each goal—spelling out exactly what will be done, by whom, by when, how successful achievement will be measured, and what good performance looks like—the more accountable you are making the person or persons who will carry it out.

Without a clear accountability system, people will not know where to focus their energy. This must be established during performance planning.

SYSTEM NO. 2: DATA/INFORMATION

Clear goals tell people not only what they are accountable for, but also what good performance looks like. This second aspect of goal setting requires an operating data/information system. It is not only important in performance planning but is essential in performance monitoring and feedback.

Given today's explosion of information, managing and disseminating information can itself become a key strategy. When we talk about data systems, we're talking about ways to get people information on finances, customer feedback, performance—anything that supports them in effective decision making or coaching. People without pertinent information cannot self-monitor, coach and recognize others, or make sound decisions; people with information can.

> **If you can't measure something,**
> **you can't manage it.**
> **If you can't measure something,**
> **you can't coach it.**
> **If you can't measure something,**
> **you can't recognize it.**

SYSTEM NO. 3: TRAINING

Training is a key strategy when it comes to making any company a learning organization. After unclear goals, the second most common reason people fail in their jobs is lack of training. We've already talked about training and its importance. While initial training is important after people have been hired, ongoing training is necessary to keep them relevant and motivated. When people are not performing well, it's either a can't-do problem or a won't-do problem—or both. Training is perfect for can't-do problems. As we've implied earlier, won't-do problems are not training issues but personal or organizational culture issues. When people's poor performance is both a can't-do and won't-do problem, career planning might be appropriate.

SYSTEM NO. 4: FEEDBACK

Performance monitoring and feedback are the guts of performance management. As I've said before, feedback is the breakfast of champions. I first heard that saying from a colleague, Rick Tate, who is an expert in customer service training. Can you imagine trying out for the Olympics as a sprinter and then the timer refuses to give you your times? What about a high jumper who doesn't know how high he or she has jumped? Without feedback people have no way of knowing whether performance is on the mark or falling short.

One of my favorite examples is bowling. Have you ever watched people bowl? If after rolling the ball they jump up and down and scream and yell, what's happened? They got a strike. They knocked down all the pins. Unfortunately, many organizations have a different form of bowling. The bowler gets ready and looks down the alley but there are no pins. How long would you want to bowl without any pins?

When you tell people they've got to give their folks feedback on results, they often set up a second form of bowling. Now when the bowler looks down the alley, there are pins set up, but there's a sheet across the pins. When he or she rolls the ball, it goes through the sheet. They hear a crack, but they don't know how many they knocked down. You ask, "How'd you do?" and they say, "I don't know. It felt okay." They didn't get any feedback.

When you insist that people need feedback, very often a third form of bowling is set up. Now when the bowler approaches, he or she looks down the alley and sees the sheet is still hiding the pins, but now there's a new element in the game. Behind the sheet is a supervisor. The bowler rolls the ball down the alley, it goes through the sheet, they hear a crack and then the supervisor holds up two fingers. "You knocked down two." In a lot of organizations they wouldn't say, "You've knocked down two." They'd say, "You missed eight." What you've got to do is take the sheet away and let your people see the pins so they can observe how many they knocked down. Feedback really is the breakfast of champions. Relevant feedback is important for problem identification, coaching, and performance evaluation.

SYSTEM NO. 5: RECOGNITION

Recognition is critical to sustaining good performance. It plays a major role in performance evaluation. There are two aspects of recognition. The first has to do with catching people doing things right as they happen. The second is rewarding people's performance over time. If you understand the difference between these two aspects, you will see why recognition is also important for performance monitoring and feedback. Feedback should be an ongoing thing that's given to people as soon after they perform as possible. It should be immediate and specific, otherwise it's not useful to people. When we talk about recognition, we're talking about rewarding people's performance over time with plaques, money, and so on.

Both aspects of recognition are important. If you wait to recognize people's performance until the end of the year, they could get discouraged. Nobody seems to be noticing their good efforts. If football fans only cheered when their team scored, teams might never score. Encouragement along the way keeps them focused on their goals. At the end of the season if the team has been successful, an awards banquet recognizes their achievement. That will motivate them for the next season.

In the world of work, a good recognition system is invaluable for compensation and promotion decisions and praising people's behavior over time.

Following up on good intentions is not always easy. It's the systems you set up that keep people on track and make sure that good performance follows.

YUM!'S REALITY: GETTING PEOPLE WIRED IN WITH THE RIGHT SYSTEMS AND PROCESSES

*In business you get traction by winning,
not just by doing things nice.*

—David Novak

While David Novak is out to build a Customer Mania culture where people come first, he is careful to preserve the passion for excellence and the drive for bottom-line results that had been strong at PepsiCo. By keeping both people and results foremost, the company works not only at motivating their workforce and driving results, but also at increasing retention and decreasing turnover.

Executional Excellence
We beat the year-ago results by continuously improving and innovating. We follow through with daily intensity.

Rob Savage, chief operating officer of Taco Bell, says, "This whole cultural thing is not just about everybody feeling great about themselves. It's not about, 'Well, if profits go up, fine, if they don't, well, that's all right, too.' No. Part of this culture is *wanting to win.* Winning today ultimately means you have to drive sales and profitability. You do that by taking great care of your people and your customers."

"This isn't just the warm, fuzzy stuff without the hard part," Savage adds. "We believe in excellence. We believe in accountability and the kind of coaching that elevates people to achieve that accountability. Those things are also key parts. So, bottom line? The culture should be the enabler, the facilitator that allows you to achieve performance above and beyond the norm. If it doesn't, then there's something wrong with it. It's that simple."

MEASURES ARE A KEY TO THE CUSTOMER MANIA CULTURE

The belief that "if you can't measure it, you can't manage it" is a given. Yum! has a rigorous system of measures in place to identify opportunities to coach, recognize, and reward people. They are passionate not only about measuring outcomes but just as importantly, measuring progress. Without measures, they would be unable to maintain their balance between people and results.

Accountability
We do what we say, we are accountable,
we act like owners.

Measures are about a lot more than accountability. In fact, measures are a key to the Customer Mania culture, for they provide the means to recognize both progress and outcomes.

Systems and processes are not sexy—but they're imperative to making everything work. Without process and standards, there is no way a company can effectively operate in 100 countries around the world.

CHAMPS: A WAY OF KEEPING SCORE

Many of the great ideas that catch on companywide are things that start somewhere within the organization. Others recognize it and then it spreads. A great example of this is CHAMPS, the operating measuring system developed by the Yum! international team.

CHAMPS was a way to bring consistency across the company in terms of how each restaurant measures success. **C**leanliness, **H**ospitality, **A**ccuracy, **M**aintenance, **P**roduct Quality, and **S**peed with Service are all things every restaurant team member can relate to. Yum! quickly branded CHAMPS with a whole host of training and recognition programs.

"While CHAMPS is a measure of the restaurant from the customer's perspective, it gets pretty deep into the restaurant operations that produce the customer outcomes," says Kathy Gosser, senior director of global CHAMPS. "We have three measures at the restaurant level that are based on CHAMPS: CHAMPSCheck, CHAMPS Excellence Review (CER), and the Hot Line.

"CHAMPSCheck is an assessment of the restaurant directly from the customer's (mystery shopper's) point of view using an instrument based on CHAMPS. In one form or another every restaurant gets evaluated once or twice a month. (Pizza Hut restaurants get evaluated sixteen times a month.) The results are used to recognize and reward performance, and to identify opportunities and get them fixed.

"The people we call operations and recognition specialists do CHAMPS Excellence Reviews. About three times a year they make unannounced coaching sessions at every restaurant, company, and franchisee. Good restaurants have fewer reviews; ones with opportunities get more. These are three- to four-hour evaluation and coaching visits.

"They don't just go in and tell you what's wrong," Kathy says. "They identify opportunities and have a computer program that automatically prints out an action plan with responsibilities and timelines—here's what's going on and here is how you fix it. This is a very hands-on, workable tool for RGMs."

Talking to Kathy, we began to see how the CHAMPS system—like everything else at this company—contributes to the culture of recognition.

"The action plan can be tailored to individual conditions. Most importantly, the coaching session identifies opportunities for recognition—that's why they are called operations *and* recognition specialists. They are responsible not only for finding out opportunities for improvement, but for identifying what's going right and reinforcing it. There is always something to recognize."

The company's mentality around performance scores is one we hadn't encountered before. It is saying to people, "We want to coach you, then measure your performance—*so that we can recognize you.*" The company is unique in that it makes use of people's need for recognition while in the very process of dealing with low performance. It's a perfect example of the company's both/and philosophy—both people and results.

Kathy made it clear that accountability is built in both ways. "In return, the specialists are evaluated by RGMs on the quality of the visit. Was it a fair evaluation? Did they explain the action plan? Did they recognize people? Was value added in coaching and training? The basic job responsibility of the CHAMPS and recognition specialist is to coach and provide recognition. These RGM evaluations make up 15 percent of the specialist's performance review.

"The third source of customer feedback is our 1-800 hotline. It provides a safety net to make sure we take care of all our customers.

They call in with both concerns and compliments. Complaints are given to the RGM quickly so we can recover; we want the opportunity to save the customer's loyalty. The brands also use this for feedback on new products and promotions. It's a great early warning system."

BRINGING CHAMPS TO LIFE

Jacquelyn Bollman, a KFC area coach in Louisville, talks about how CHAMPS really comes to life in the restaurant:

"We have what is called a CHAMPSCheck, where twice every month someone comes in like a customer—we don't know who or when—and evaluates our restaurants on things like cleanliness, hot and fresh food, and customer service. Each store gets rated on a scale from 0 to 100. If there is a piece of paper in the parking lot, we get dinged. The restaurant gets an overall score and the team member who serves the mystery shopper has a big impact on the score."

What's fascinating is that the CHAMPSCheck ratings are hardwired into recognition. "When the store gets a 100," Bollman continues, "I go right over there and give the team members a big hug and a prize. Yesterday we got our scores in. One restaurant got a 96; it would have gotten a 100, but the counter person was wearing a visor, and didn't have a hair net. A&W got a 97, two restaurants got 100s, and then I had one store that got a 77 when the cashier forgot to say hello. Some coaching needed there!

"You've got to hold people accountable, but at the same time you've got to have fun. When A&W got that 97, I called up the cashier and ribbed him: 'I'm going to kill you! Everything else was perfect! The food was hot, the parking lot was immaculate, and the lobby was sparkling! If you just had said, *Would you like a dessert?* You know better!' I could do this because this guy knows I know he's a winner. For instance, our Combo-Plus is a big menu sale to a customer, and he is a guy that combo-pluses the hell out of people."

BALANCING THE SCORECARD

The Balanced Scorecard is used to provide an overall assessment of the restaurant. It has what are called the four buckets: Customers, People, Sales, and Profits. The customer bucket is assessed by CHAMPS and the mystery shopper. A Founder's Survey at above-store level and a Voice of Champions survey in the restaurant gives the company a good idea of how folks are feeling and how the store is doing.

"People want to feel like they're part of a bigger enterprise," David Novak says. "They don't want to go to work and just be a cook or a drive-through service team member, they want to be a part of a team. As a part of a team, they have a much higher calling. The Balanced Scorecard helps them feel that, because it's a simple way for the entire team to know how it is doing."

By now you can see how Yum! wires in accountability; at the same time, you can see the values in play. The company uses detailed measures on key business result areas—starting with the customer—and then balances it out with people, sales, and profits. However, the measures are anything but the old whack-and-disappear routine: coaching and recognition come right along with the measures. This is a formula for developing winners.

"The key to balancing people with results," says Scott Bergren, chief marketing and food innovation officer at KFC/Yum!, "is back-up—systems that ensure that leaders can stay focused on both ends of the beam. Some of the more complicated enterprises to run are retail restaurant stores. Real tough. I mean, the discipline of running these stores—hitting your numbers, while helping your employees value their jobs and having customers appreciate the entire experience—is no easy matter. In most restaurant organizations profitability and discipline are the first things that have to be learned. The last things are usually the things *we* think are the heart of the business: recognition, customers, employee attitude—in short, putting people first.

"It's when I know I'm disciplined and practiced enough at running my business that I can really start to address the more important parts of the business, which is taking care of my people and taking care of my customers. You can't do that unless you have reliable systems in place that are going on automatically on the results side."

Like so many others at Yum!, Bergren speaks passionately about his work. What's interesting is that he suggests that his love of this business comes out of precisely that tension between people and profits. "I love this business," he says. "I don't think there's any greater calling, because at the same time that we are paying close attention to the nuts and bolts of running restaurants, we're growing and developing our people. Often team members come to us with problems, with low self-esteem, with not a great outlook. People have told them that they don't count. What we tell them is just the opposite: 'We really respect what you're doing. You can have a career in our business. We can show you so many people that started out exactly where you are and have built a great life for themselves.' Taking care of people—it's hidden gold."

RACKING AND STACKING

You'd think that going public with people's performance scores would decrease motivation and morale and build unhealthy competition. That would be true in the average human organization. However, Yum! has a unique system of publicizing scores that reduces blame and builds motivation. They call it racking and stacking. Racking and stacking is the practice of openly sharing people's performance scores. It's usually done by posting a list of everybody's CHAMPS ratings, from best to worst. They check the measure of

CHAMPSCheck results, and every store is ranked. So is every region, every store, every area coach.

Chief people officer Anne Byerlein told us, "We work with the people who are not performing well and coach them for success. We give them the tools and attention to improve their performance and the ongoing feedback to get better and better. On the other hand, we publicly recognize those who are doing really well and those who have made significant improvement, so everybody will aspire to be winners. We've gotten better at doing this. We used to recognize only a few top performers or teams, but that wasn't enough to make a big impact. Now we have a results-based culture where recognition is a natural part of doing business and not an add-on."

In the last couple of years the company has focused on recognizing not just perfection but improvement. They want to keep people moving up, and they realize that it's just as important to call attention to what people are getting better at as it is to recognize their best. Racking and stacking clearly results in improvement, Rob Savage tells us. "We've found the practice really does drive performance. The intent is to make performance public, from the top to the bottom. Everybody here wants to be the best. When a rack-and-stack comes out and you're not at the top, it motivates you to keep pushing. You want your team to be at the top.

"People might think this practice would work to humiliate people. In some business cultures it could wreak havoc. But it doesn't in our culture. In fact, people ranked at the top think, 'How can I help those at the bottom? I want to stay here at the top, but how can I get them over the wall?' You'll hear that phrase, 'getting over the wall,' a lot around here. It means being at least up to standard on the Balanced Scorecard. RGMs say, 'I had to get over the wall. Now I want to get to the top.' "

One of the strongest trends we see in Yum! is healthy internal competition. Improvements from the racking and stacking— increased motivation to win, and even to help others—are excellent examples of the payoff in results from building a people-first culture. The trust Yum! builds enables it to require more of its people.

In most companies where recognition is scarce or absent and where blame and lack of ongoing coaching is the expected result of doing poorly, managers wouldn't dare use public ratings like these. But in an environment where you know that your boss and everyone else is on your side and wants you to win, getting a low score doesn't shame you, it makes you want to improve.

By having very powerful measures in place, Yum! is able to feel the pulse of their restaurants so they can intervene and coach on an ongoing basis. By racking and stacking, Yum! frequently makes clear how people are performing and what their challenges are, so they can fix what needs fixing. They don't have to wait until the end of the year to find out they screwed up on something six months ago because their manager kept the feedback in reserve in case it was needed to fit them someplace down in the normal distribution curve compensation.

COMPENSATION AND "OWNERSHIP"

Now we've got you measured, racked, and stacked. Time to put more motivation into the brew. Like other systems, Yum!'s compensation program is a function of its people-first culture. Gregg Dedrick used the phrase "capturing their hearts and minds" more than once as he described the company's methods of rewarding people. Far from merely paying off people, compensation is strategically designed to enlist their commitment to the company's values.

"Out of the box at Tricon," Dedrick relates, "we said we wanted to create a company where people felt like owners. This was about creating the right long-term company; we wanted folks to be committed to its success, so we tied compensation to their commitment. We asked everybody on the senior management level to agree that within five years they would meet certain ownership guidelines where they had to buy a certain amount of stock outright. Everybody on David's team within the first five years had to buy a million dollars worth of Tricon stock—not counting the options—this is stuff they had to purchase.

"At the director level, they had to buy Tricon stock out of their own pocket. If they didn't buy it, or weren't at that level, they didn't get the full stock option grant. Our message is that we really want people to feel like they have skin in the game, and if they're not committed to this business, they need to leave. One way to get people's passion and commitment is by saying, 'Hey, we're going to grow this business *together,* and we're here for the long run.'"

At Yum! the RGM is number one. The company's leaders didn't want that phrase to be merely lip service. Stock options are one of the ways the company shows its appreciation for the RGM. They give U.S.-based RGMs and many foreign-based RGMs stock options, an initial option grant of $5,000 of Yum! stock. RGMs have the opportunity to earn an additional $15,000 Yum! stock option grant, based upon their performance in growing their restaurant profits year over year. "It's a great opportunity," says Dedrick. "There are a lot of different ways you can measure different things, but we needed to keep that one pretty simple. We just said, 'Year over year if you have more sales and more profits, you get rewarded.'"

Dedrick adds, "At the restaurant level you can squeeze profits but you can't squeeze sales because you really have to stay customer focused. So we got focused on the top line, as well as profits. We had two goals for everybody—grow their sales and grow their profits. At the end of the year we have prizes and rewards for the whole restaurant team."

PAY FOR PERFORMANCE

Yum! puts a great deal of emphasis on pay for performance, what is called "variable pay." (You know they love you but hey, you've got to perform.) A percentage of your compensation is based on bonuses and the further you go up the organization, the bigger the percentage. If you are an RGM you go for what is called the target bonus—$5,000, give or take. Basing the variable part, or bonus, on performance on your blue chip ties compensation into line-of-sight, top to bottom.

In most organizations, if you perform well you get 3 percent and if you don't perform well you don't have to change—unless you're at the top. Yum! compensation is tied to improvement: if you do well, your compensation goes up; if you do poorly, it goes down. As you progress through the organization, more of your compensation is pushed over to the variable side, 15, 20, 25 percent and higher. The higher you go, the bigger the risk—and the bigger the potential reward. At the top, more than half of your compensation could be variable.

If you're at the top of the Yum! organization, the majority of your bonus is based on team performance (team defined as Yum! or brand, depending where you are located). If you're the president of Taco Bell and you had a bad year, the majority of your bonus is going to get hammered. Since the remainder of your bonus is based on your blue chips, you're probably going to take a really big hit there, too.

The further down you go in the organization, the less ability you have to impact the company's performance. Thus, your percentage of bonus based on team performance gets smaller. At the lower levels they don't want bonuses to be tied to the whole organization's. The logic is that it wouldn't be fair to hold a local RGM accountable for Taco Bell's entire national performance. Therefore we see that even in an area as internal as compensation, the company has designed its policies to focus on the customer.

YUM!'S SCORECARD

Systems and Processes

8 out of 10

EVERYONE YOU TALK TO at Yum! wants to brag about their performance coaching. We applaud their efforts in this area. But what we think makes their coaching so effective is that they have great systems and processes. Yum!'s systems provide their coaches the information they need to catch people doing things right on an ongoing basis as well as assure that their good intentions lead to appropriate behavior and desired results. The company has well-aligned tools to drive the kind of performance they're looking for. However, some of those tools are not yet reaching team members on an emotional level. Yum! still has some learning to do in the area of systems and processes, but they're well on their way to having it wired.

GET PEOPLE INSPIRED:
CREATING A RECOGNITION CULTURE

BLANCHARD'S DREAM

AFTER VISION and direction get things started, and after trained, equipped people are committed to success, how do you keep it going? By creating a recognition culture. As I said earlier, there are two aspects of recognition: one that involves catching people doing things right on a day-to-day basis and the other is recognizing people's achievement over time through a promotion, a reward, a pay raise, or something tangible. The second is important because it celebrates people's performance and long-term achievements. But the real bread-and-butter for effective managers and leaders is the day-to-day monitoring and feedback of people's performance. So let's start there.

ONGOING MONITORING AND FEEDBACK

A few years ago Jim Ballard and I wrote a book entitled *Whale Done!: The Power of Positive Relationships* with Thad Lacinak and Chuck Tompkins, two of the top trainers from Sea World who had been working with killer whales for almost thirty years. We wanted to illustrate the need for building positive relationships at work and at home. For years I've been telling managers that the key to developing people and creating great organizations is to accentuate the positive—that is, to catch people doing things right. Unfortunately, when I go around to companies and ask people how they know when they've done a good job, the most common answer I hear is, "Nobody's yelled at me lately. No news is good news."

The number one management style around the world is still what I call "seagull management." These managers aren't around until you make a mistake. Then they fly in, make a lot of noise, dump on everybody, and then fly out. As a result I decided maybe people needed a more vivid example of the power of positive relationships. I haven't found anybody who would say that it made sense to punish a killer whale and then tell trainers to get in the water with them. So if you ever go to Sea-World (and if you've never gone, go) and see a Shamu show, you'll notice there is no negative interaction between the trainers and the whales.

How do the trainers at SeaWorld get outstanding performance from killer whales with no negative interaction? They do it by accentuating the positive and redirecting inappropriate behavior. If a whale performs a routine correctly, when that whale comes back to the stage, the trainers will dump a bucket of fish down its throat, rub its tongue, hug it, or do any other positive thing they can think of. What they are saying to the whale is, "Atta boy. Atta girl. You did it right."

What do they do if a whale makes a mistake or does not perform a routine correctly? They focus no energy on the mistake. You know what they do? They redirect the whale back to either what they wanted it to do, or something else that they know the whale can do, and then they try to catch the animal doing something right. So if you go to a Shamu show and a whale comes back to the stage and the trainer gestures the whale back to the center of the pool, you know the whale didn't do it right that time and the trainer wants the whale to try again. And the animal takes off again with a desire to do it right this time. Why? Because it wants to keep those positive rein-forcements coming. Redirection refocuses energy and sets up an opportunity to accentuate the positive in the future.

How does that work with people? Focus on what you want people to do, not on what they did wrong. People want to know when they are performing well and if they are not, they want to be helped back on the right path. If someone makes a mistake, rather than focusing on what they did wrong, an effective manager will say something like, "Next time, maybe we ought to do it this way."

One caution about praising and recognition: Don't wait to acknowledge people's efforts until they have done it exactly right, otherwise you might wait forever. Remember:

Praise progress—it's a moving target.

We know that works with little kids, but we forget to use it with big people. How do you teach a child how to walk? When you stand the kid up and say, "Walk," and the kid falls down, you don't grab him and spank him. If you did, what would happen? You'd have a twenty-one-year-old kid crawling around the house. Instead, when the kid falls you pick him up and hug him and say, "You stood!" Then the next day when the kid stumbles forward and falls, you shout out, "You took your first step!" and you hug and kiss him.

How do you teach a kid how to speak? If you wanted to have a child say, "Give me a glass of water, please," you wouldn't wait until the kid said that full sentence before you gave him any water or you'd have a dead, dehydrated kid. Instead you say, "Water, water." Then when the kid says, "Laller," you get all excited and shout, "She said her first word! Get Grandmother on the phone!" When the kid gets on the phone with Grandmother and says "laller" everybody is thrilled. Now you don't want that kid at twenty-one going into restaurants asking for a glass of "laller." So after a while you only accept "water" and then you move on to "please." Again, remember to praise progress—it's a moving target. I can't say enough about accentuating the positive.

PRAISING MAKES PEOPLE AND RELATIONSHIPS STRONG

All good relationships start off on a positive vein. Then you spend time with the person and what happens? You start to notice things that displease you: annoying habits, questionable decisions. You think to yourself, *You've got to be kidding me! What's going on around here?* Pretty soon all you're doing is accentuating the negative.

This happens in the world of work, too. You get all excited about a new employee and take that person around for everyone to meet. Then after a while, you figure you've got to get back to your own job and you disappear. Then someone comes and tells you, "Do you know what that new person did?" And pretty soon you're seagulling in and starting to accentuate the negative.

I recently celebrated my fortieth anniversary with my wife, Margie. At a celebration party people asked us if we would talk about marriage. When Margie got a chance to share, she blew everyone away. She said, "You finally get a great marriage when you decide to fall in love with the total package. What you fell in love with initially, as well as the stuff that bugs you." Then she said something really powerful. "If you can love someone else like that, you have a chance of being loved that way yourself."

We all fall short of perfection. We all have our weaknesses. We all make mistakes. When people know that you are positive about them and care about them, you can even have an impact on some of their behavior that's not so positive. When feedback is coming out of support, people are better able to listen and learn.

PUTTING RECOGNITION TO WORK ON A DAY-TO-DAY BASIS

Recognition works best in organizations where the traditional hierarchal pyramid is turned upside down and managers realize that their people are responsible and it's their job to be responsive to their needs and to help them win. That signals commitment from the top managers to make recognition an integral part of the culture.

One way to do that is to have an Employee of the Moment program—not to be confused with Employee of the Month programs. Employee of the Month programs are real duck activities. If you've ever attended an Employee of the Month meeting, you probably heard people saying things like: "Your department won last month; we can't have the same department win two months in a row—quack, quack." Or "she's been very loyal, and nobody's recognized her—quack, quack." If you want to hear a real quacker, go to an Employee of the Year meeting. That's a real winner. I've always felt it doesn't make much sense to pick out only one person. What I believe in is Employee of the Moment. I love to see companies set up an office called The Eagle's Nest. If anybody gets caught—by either an internal or external customer—going the extra mile and creating a raving fan, a call is immediately made to this office. The Eagle's Nest dispatches someone with a Polaroid camera to see if they can catch the eagle in flight. The person is recognized on the spot. Often, a wall of fame is established, where employees' pictures and eagle stories are displayed.

In our company, my official title is Chief Spiritual Officer. My major role is cheerleading people and keeping our vision and values alive. Every morning I leave a voice mail for our two-hundred-fifty-plus people from the United States, Canada, and the United Kingdom. In those messages I do three things: First, I tell people when someone needs our prayers. Our folks call me about themselves, their families, and other important people in their lives. Having done this for almost ten years, we have some real evidence about the power of prayer. Second, I catch people doing things right. People send me stories about our folks going the extra mile not only for our clients but for each other. People love to be caught doing something right. Finally, I leave an inspirational message around our operating values of integrity, relationships, success, and learning. I mention this because I think when it comes to catching people doing things right and reinforcing the importance of your values, it doesn't hurt saying it over and over and over again. I ask people all the time, "How many of you are sick and tired of all the compliments you get at work?" They all laugh. We can never get enough.

RECOGNITION AS A CELEBRATION
OF PERFORMANCE OVER TIME

While people love to be caught doing something right as soon after they do it as possible, they also love to be recognized for their long-term performance. People love a party. Celebrating and recognizing people's performance at the end of the year or after a time that required high commitment and hard work energizes them and gets them excited about future good performance. Most companies have awards banquets and special occasions when they honor their high achievers. These can be very special occasions. People dress up in their best and applaud each other's contributions.

At our company, we take it one step further. We not only recognize top achievers, but we celebrate people living our values. Annually we have a Week of Excellence that brings everyone to San Diego to meet, greet, and plan the future. The highlight of that week is our People's Choice Awards. These are awards voted on by everyone in the company to acknowledge special efforts people have made to walk our talk. For example, we give the Mother Teresa Award to the person who has reached out to serve and minister to others. The Martin Luther King Award recognizes a person who embodies our values. The Patch Adams Award goes to the person who is the most fun to work with. The Timex Manager of the Year goes to someone who has accomplished on time an important task under difficult circumstances. We give a Raving Fan Award for a person who continually goes the extra mile for our customers. We also give an internal Raving Fan Award for the person who is always ready to serve a colleague in need. The One Minute Manager award goes to the person identified as our most effective servant leader. The highlight of our People's Choice Awards is our Most Value-Led Player. This is the person during the last year who has made the greatest contribution to the success of our organization but has done it always with our values in mind. When each award is announced, the five finalists' pictures go up on the big screen. When the winner is announced, the place erupts in applause, tears, hugs, and high fives.

Don't underestimate the power of recognition for long-term performance. If you put your people first and recognize their efforts, they will put your customers first. It's that simple.

YUM!'S REALITY: CREATING A RECOGNITION CULTURE

DAVID NOVAK AND THE YUM! leadership ascribe to a basic truth about human beings:

Recognition is a universal need. People everywhere want to be appreciated.

Yum! wants to be the best in any industry at the recognition game and is counting on its culture of recognition and celebration of people to drive its business success. In fact, recognition is a part of each strategy at Yum! It is the main ingredient that differentiates and drives this unique culture. There are people in executive positions whose job is to build the recognition element of the Yum! culture. The goal is to have *people at all levels recognizing people.*

Recognition
*We find reasons to celebrate the achievements
of others and have fun doing it.*

When organizations approach recognition programmatically, it becomes little more than lip service, and often becomes a joke. (A stand-up comedian recently got a big laugh when he said that winning an employee-of-the-month award is "like being a winner for being a loser.") Anne Byerlein, Yum!'s chief people officer, says that when she was put in charge of recognition at the new company, it didn't take her long to realize this was much more than a program. It was about changing a culture.

From the outset Yum! leaders have believed that their secret ingredient—the one that would reduce turnover, build retention, and ultimately drive Customer Mania and business performance—was recognition. Consequently, the Yum! Brands culture is raising recognition to the level of an art form.

NO BEAT-UP

The leaders in Yum! don't appreciate seagull management. They like to accentuate the positive. In one Pizza Hut area coach's opinion, recognition is the most important element to cascade down an organization. Gladys Woclaw's conviction is backed by twenty years' experience.

"Back in the eighties and early nineties," she says, "when your boss came down to the store, it was a beat-up. They'd come in and tell you what was wrong, but offer no solutions to help you fix it. Now you see the president, the vice president, and other top managers coming into your restaurant with high fives and recognition, presenting the Big Cheese award to the RGM in front of the crew and taking a picture. Everybody's treated like an individual and recognized for the great things they're doing. Wow, we've come such a long way."

WHAT DOES IT MEAN TO RECOGNIZE SOMEONE?

For Charles Whittaker, KFC franchisee in the United Kingdom, recognition is "a lot of things. It can mean just picking a person out in a crowd, or remembering a familiar face. Greeting, saying hello, thanking someone, or otherwise acknowledging them, are all ways of showing recognition.

"For many or most of our new hires at the restaurant team member level, it's their first job. It's also low-paying and the fast-food industry traditionally has a high turnover rate. Most come from low-income situations, where giving deserved praise and recognition is most likely rarely experienced. The great majority of people who come to work for this, the largest restaurant company in the world, have never in their lives had anyone tell them they've done a good job with anything. So the first form of recognition-giving that is very meaningful for people is assigning them a task to do, and then telling them they did it well."

ONGOING RECOGNITION

When it comes to catching people doing things right and recognizing their good performance on the spot, coaching is the main vehicle at Yum! Rather than catching people doing things wrong, the company's coaches are more interested in accentuating the positive. When mistakes are made, rather than focus energy on what went wrong, they use it as an opportunity to coach. Why? One of their core values is Belief in People.

When Taco Bell president Emil Brolick speaks about the workforce, it's with respect and generosity: "I believe the vast majority of people out there have a lot of pride and self-esteem and they want to do a great job serving our customers. That commitment needs to be constantly recognized and supported. The way team members respond to and take care of a guest is a function of how those team members feel about themselves. If they have a lot of pride in themselves, they're going to take pride in what they do; they're going to care how they present themselves. Obviously, our customers are going to see that. It's our job to make absolutely sure that we have the kind of RGM and environment in our restaurants that fosters team member self-esteem, pride, and a feeling that each member is making some kind of a difference.

"Every corporation out there is faced with this issue. They're all essentially in the people business, whether they know it or not. The business we're in is a real dramatization of that; you have all of these little manufacturing plants out there called restaurants, but this is not a product that's being turned out and put on the shelf. The reason it's so people-dependent is that the quality-control opportunities exist in small moments in time. In a way, we are the most people-dependent kind of organization, which I think begs for some kind of a deep belief in a culture."

Senior vice president of public affairs Jonathan Blum believes that recognition is the key to creating a Customer Mania culture worldwide and the ingredient that can elevate the company to greatness:

"We want each person we recognize to be thinking, 'I can't wait to find someone doing something right so that I can recognize them, too.' You want to pass it on because you know the power of what that recognition meant to you. Think what it would mean for each person who has been recognized personally to pay it forward to two, three, ten, or twenty people. That's when it becomes a real and living part of your daily mindset. When you've got everyone doing that in an organization, it helps take you from being a good company to a great one."

REWARDING PERFORMANCE OVER TIME

While people like to be caught doing something right on a day-to-day basis, they like their demonstrated skills to be recognized as well. Charles Whittaker describes two additional modes of recognition besides acknowledging people on the spot for a job well done:

"Recognizing people also means involving them in the business, showing them how it works, engaging them creatively, using their ideas. This makes them feel important; there is a sense of ownership reflected in the things they do. Promoting people from within is also a powerful form of recognition. Not only does the person being promoted feel good, this causes other team members to say, 'Hey, if I work hard, I could get there too.'"

In addition to involving people in the business and promoting from within, a major form of recognition is to celebrate people's performance over time. The folks at Yum! are experts at this.

PASS THE FLOPPY CHICKEN

Seldom—if ever—have we seen an organization make better use of language, myth, and symbols than Yum! does. The Floppy Chicken is a stellar example.

As the new president of KFC in 1994, David Novak was looking for a way to break through the organizational clutter. He wanted a recognition award, a signature item that people would value. He wanted to demonstrate everywhere he went that—as he says—"People will do what you appreciate." He also wanted something fun that would get attention.

With the help of KFC head coach Steve Provost, he came up with the now famous Floppy Chicken, the sort of ridiculous fake plucked fowl one associates with stand-up comedy. When Provost told him, "You have to make it personal," Novak instituted the process of writing a comment about what the person had achieved right on the chicken, and numbering each one of them like the collector's items they were. (He also gave the person a hundred dollars because, as he put it, "You can't eat a rubber chicken.")

The weirdness of the award became a part of its appeal. The fun-and-foolishness aspect was important to Novak as he went around the company presenting this award to top performers in KFC. As he says, "I didn't want to give a watch or a plaque; I wanted to shock the system. I wanted everybody to say, 'Hey you know what, this guy's a little different. I mean he's different from the last president that was in here. Things are really going to be different. He's shaking things up here.'"

Instead of using emotional rewards to induce compliance, Yum! leaders use them to generate excitement. Roger Eaton, managing director of South Pacific operations, explains: "When you recognize somebody, it holds up a certain behavior and helps that person understand that's what you really want from them. Plus, when you recognize someone you create an incentive for everybody in that place to repeat that behavior; they want to be recognized, too. So you've generated a vision of where you're going, you've created the excitement behind getting there, and you've brought fun and energy into the room."

Recognition is your secret weapon as a leader.

—Gregg Dedrick

If you visit Yum!'s Restaurant Support Center (the "White House") in Louisville, you will soon find yourself in the Walk of Champions, a brightly colored hallway lined with pictures honoring people for their achievements. The hall connects the offices and the cafeteria, so employees are continuously passing through it. Shirlie Kunimoto, vice president of operations excellence, told us, "Walking through there, you just feel good."

The Walk of Champions is lined with a dazzling display of recognition awards from all around the world. Every leader at Yum! is required to have a personal award. What the award is, however, is up to each individual. People get very creative and tend to design awards that reward behavior they value. Each award is tailored to a specific achievement; each is a testament to delightful creativity.

WHO'S THE BULLDOG?

Chuck Rawley, chief development officer, provides a perfect example of someone who devised a personalized award. In the days just following David Novak's coming on board, Chuck accompanied him on a tour of the facilities in Las Vegas. On the plane ride home, they had a heated discussion of what the next steps were for the company. David was pushing for fixing the facilities; Chuck was pushing to "get the food right."

"I ranked the facilities low," said Chuck. "Food was a more pressing problem. I disagreed with David and wouldn't let go. We went back and forth, back and forth. Both of us are pretty strong people.

"I hung in there, even though I thought I was probably putting my job on the line. Then David said, 'You know, Chuck, you're a persistent bulldog. You won't give up your point. You just chew and chew on something.'

"So I turned the bulldog into my personal recognition award. It's the hood ornament for Mack trucks. It represents tenacity, courage, loyalty, and consistency."

Here is just a partial list of other awards that line the Hall of Champions:

RECOGNITION AWARDS

The Platinum Tray Award
The Fish Award
Helping Hand Award
Aztec Arrow Award
The Good Scout Award
High Four Award
Chain of Champions Award
Mirror Award
Knockout Marketing Award
2 Million RGM Celebration Award
Team Passion Award
Pizza Hut Gold Award
Golden Whistle Award
Team Excellence Award
Making Cents Award
Leo Award
The A-Team Award
KFC Best of the Best Award
People Magnet Award
The Way of the Paddle Award
The Game Ball Award
The Golden Shopping Cart Award
RGMs Award
Lighthouse Award
The CHAMPS 100 Club Award

(continued on following page)

The Detail Award
The Torch Award
The Golden Bell Award
Leaders Top Radio Award
Whatever It Takes Award
Radical Rooster Award
Magnified Customer Mania
Bulldozer Award
Fasten Your Seatbelt Award
Customer Mania Award
Silver Spoon Award
Bull Dog Award
ANTZ Award
Bringing Home the Bacon Award
Perfect Peach Award
Mission Impossible Award
The Big Cheese Award
Order of the Brick Award
The Golden Glove Award
Golden Wishbone Award

If you spend more time in the building you will likely hear cheers breaking out at unexpected times. "It's okay to disturb everyone with a Yum! cheer," Kunimoto says. "Another thing that will get your attention is the Recognition Band." She's referring to a group of workers who play instruments and volunteer to be called together anytime to go and honor someone for something. Says Kunimoto, "It's a visceral part of our company."

RECOGNITION CREATES PASSION
AROUND THE WORLD

Peter Hearl, president of Pizza Hut and former executive vice president of Yum! Restaurants International, spearheaded driving the one-system culture all around the world based on Yum!'s *How We Work Together* principles. When other people were saying, "My country is different," Peter was adamant that these principles were universal. Early on, he encouraged David Novak to make them global. Peter has seen the difference recognition can make in markets all across the globe:

"In-Soo Cho, Korea's managing director, developed a smiling pizza face as his recognition award. Art Rautio, who runs the Asia franchise support team, developed a Tiger Award, because the tiger is such a big part of Asian culture. Roger Eaton, who runs the Australia and New Zealand businesses, developed the Mission Impossible Award, which is basically a little lead bomb with a fuse on it, inspired by the TV show *Mission Impossible.* Irfan Mustafa in the Middle East has got a very elaborate brass and bronze Golden Camel Award."

Hearl concludes, "No matter what race, religion, color, creed, country, or background, people have a desire to be recognized for work well done. Particularly in the restaurant business, they want to feel like they're part of an extended family. This stuff works all across the world."

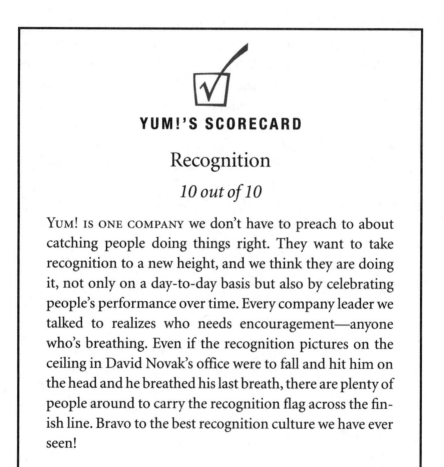

YUM!'S SCORECARD

Recognition

10 out of 10

YUM! IS ONE COMPANY we don't have to preach to about catching people doing things right. They want to take recognition to a new height, and we think they are doing it, not only on a day-to-day basis but also by celebrating people's performance over time. Every company leader we talked to realizes who needs encouragement—anyone who's breathing. Even if the recognition pictures on the ceiling in David Novak's office were to fall and hit him on the head and he breathed his last breath, there are plenty of people around to carry the recognition flag across the finish line. Bravo to the best recognition culture we have ever seen!

GIVE PEOPLE OPPORTUNITIES TO GROW: CAREER PLANNING THE RIGHT WAY

BLANCHARD'S DREAM

ONE OF THE BIGGEST NEEDS people have is for growth and development. After becoming experts in particular jobs, very often they start looking for new challenges. This is where career planning comes in. If you can enrich their present jobs with additional responsibilities, you might still be able to challenge them, but if that's not possible, then what other opportunities are available to them in the organization?

My own belief is that people should not be promoted or provided a new opportunity until they've done two things. First, they've done a really good job of what you've asked them to do. Second, they have trained someone who can take their place. So often I've seen people who are not doing a good job in their present position wanting to be given new opportunities. I'm all for career planning and making sure that people are in a job that builds on their strengths, but unless you have determined that they are in the wrong spot, performance should precede promotion opportunities.

In terms of preparing a ready replacement, team contribution is an important citizenship requirement. You don't want to create an environment where everybody is competing with each other; you want an environment where they're all helping, supporting, and encouraging each other to be the best.

As I indicated earlier, a lot of managers still believe they need to use a normal distribution curve, to grade a few people high, a few people low, and the rest of the people average. Getting the wrong people off the team is not intended to get rid of an arbitrary percentage of people. Ideally, through coaching and working with people, they can all succeed. If your people win, the organization should win if their goals and objectives can impact business results. Everyone's work should either impact business results or support someone who does.

If you make every effort to help people win and they still don't—yet they have the right character and are modeling your vision and values—you have to look at career planning. These people are probably in the wrong spots for their strengths. Career planning is not only important for good people who might be in the wrong position, but also for good performers who want to be challenged and continue to enrich their jobs and take on more responsibility.

One of the reasons people often are reluctant to discard the normal distribution curve is that they don't know how they will deal with career planning if some people don't get sorted out at a lower level. If a high percentage of people are top performers, they wonder how firms can possibly reward them all. As people move up the hierarchy, aren't there fewer opportunities for promotion? I believe that question is quite naive. If you treat people well and help them win in their present position, they often use their creativity to come up with new business ideas that will expand your vision and eventually grow the organization. Protecting the hierarchy doesn't do your people or your organization any good. I'll never forget the story that Ralph Stayer, co-author with Jim Belasco of *The Flight of the Buffalo*, tells. His secretary came to him one time with a great idea for a new business. He was in the sausage manufacturing business. She suggested that they start a catalog business, because at the time they were only selling their sausages directly to grocery stores and other distributors. He said, "What a great idea! Why don't you organize a business plan and run it?" So in a short period of time his former secretary was running a major new division of his company and creating all kinds of job opportunities for people as well as revenue for the company.

YUM!'S REALITY: CAREER PLANNING

WITH A COMPANY that's growing and blowing like Yum! there are going to be a lot of opportunities for growth and development. As a result, career planning is top-of-mind for everyone, not only for their own careers but for the careers of their coworkers as well.

Belief in People
We believe in people, trust in positive intentions, encourage ideas from everyone, and actively develop a workforce that is diverse in style and background.

A PIECE OF THE DREAM

Faith and trust in people's inherent desire and ability to do well is the basis of Yum!'s crusade to keep their team members longer and to have an impact on their lives. President and chief multibranding and operating officer Aylwin Lewis says, "In general, it's not your middle-class teenagers who are getting part- and full-time jobs with us during and after high school. It's disadvantaged kids who can't find alternatives. It's people who have come here from other countries, trying to find a reasonable life for themselves and their families. It's all kinds of people who can't find a better alternative.

"This organization is committed to creating an environment in our restaurants where people like these—people who wouldn't otherwise have had the chance—can create choice in their lives. If it's their first job, they can learn skills that will serve them whatever they do long-term. They are encouraged to further their educations and are provided with tuition reimbursement to do so. If they stay, they have opportunities to grow and develop, learn new skills, develop a mindset, and get exposed to a set of values that will serve them all their lives. They have the opportunity to move on up through the organization, to build a better life for themselves and their families. And if they go elsewhere, they have been enriched by their experience."

And all because somebody believed in them.

PASSING IT ON

Roman Saenz, Pizza Hut region coach for Fort Worth, expresses deep satisfaction as he tells about the people who have progressed under his management.

"After I'd done all the hourly jobs and was promoted to RGM," said Saenz, "it felt good seeing other people coming up behind me. In my twenty-year career with Pizza Hut, I've probably promoted fifteen to twenty shift managers to assistant managers, and then on to RGMs. Two of the people I trained are area coaches today."

HELPING EACH OTHER GET AHEAD

Belief in people goes beyond restaurant operations. Debbie Hirst, KFC RGM in Louisville, tells this story: "I've been working for KFC for twenty-four years, twenty-two years as an RGM and nineteen years in this store. I've seen them come and I've seen them go; seen things I've liked and things I didn't like, I'm telling ya.

"My past two area coaches have been great. Kathy Gosser, who is now director of operations and recognition, was my area coach before Jacquelyn Bollman. Kathy is a real bombshell. She remotivated me as an RGM. I had been through some hard times, my mother died and other stuff. She tried to get to know me first before getting to be my boss. She said to me point blank, 'I don't know you, and you don't know me, so let's talk.' I shared stuff about me and she shared stuff about her. I'd never had anybody do that before. She made me want to do better for her, because of how much I respected and liked her.

"Then I got Jacquelyn Bollman, my current coach. She motivated me to get ahead. We have this new multibrand, a KFC-Long John Silver's combo opening near here, and I'm going to take it over in December. Nobody thought I was ever going to leave this restaurant. They said, 'You're lying, you're not moving, you're not leaving.' I said, 'I've been here for twenty-four years, it's time for me to move on.'

"I probably wouldn't have done it, were it not for Jacquelyn's faith in me. She kept at me: 'Are you going to be an RGM for the rest of your life? Don't you want to do something else?' We had a discussion of what I could do and she said that the way to open up my options is to run a multibrand. I got excited about the challenge. Jacquelyn told me that I needed to change some of my behavior. She was the first person to give me straight feedback and then help me get better. I've always been real straight with people, but it came across pretty hard. I've learned how to soften up and at the same time to keep my expectations high. So when this opportunity opened up, I was ready for it.

"I know this is going to be a real big challenge for me. I have never run a Long John Silver's or a multibrand, but I know the restaurant business. I understand that a multibrand is a lot more complex business to run. I wouldn't do it if it weren't for Jacquelyn. She will still be my area coach and I know she will help and support me.

"The other good thing about this change is that it opens things up for my team, lets them grow. I helped one woman who used to be a shift manager to become assistant unit manager and now she's an RGM. I've had another young man since he was sixteen years old; I helped him get to shift supervisor and now he's an assistant manager. In order for them to grow, I've got to move on. It's going to be tough to leave. My team feels like my family. I've been a coach, a parent, and a big sister. The greatest reward for me is to see people get ahead, be successful, particularly when they start out as cooks or cashiers, like I did. What I've learned is that if you don't care about them, they won't care about you."

THE WIND BENEATH MY WINGS: HAVING PEOPLE BELIEVE IN YOU

Ken Fujitani is a KFC area coach with Harman Management Corporation. Pete Harman was KFC's first franchisee, and he has played a unique leadership role in helping to bring KFC from rural America to dinner tables around the world. Harman has been instrumental in developing many of the products and marketing campaigns KFC is now famous for. The story of Ken's rise in the Harman organization echoed those of so many we talked to, people who had started out in high school or college as chicken or pizza cooks, and worked their way up. Though each of his moves up was rapid and challenging, Ken says each time it was because somebody believed in him and thought he could do it.

"Someone else would always seem to believe in you more than you believed in yourself," Ken says. "You say, 'Wow, you know what, maybe I can do this!'

"A regular part of this process is to make sure that there are people that can come up behind and under you to take over. When we settled down in our store in San Rafael and started to grow roots, we began to look at the people who worked for us not in terms of how they could help us succeed, but how we could help them have the same opportunities that we had. So we taught people the operations—how to do the paperwork, how to be responsible, how to count money, how to be part of the community.

"I didn't make this up. I got it from the people that I had worked for. I had seen it done with me. It's like a chain, something that's modeled for you, that you naturally go on and do with others. Like the RGM who helped me shape my career; that's what he did for me. Now I'm in the position where I can do that for other people. It's your responsibility at Harman's to pass on what you know and give people the same opportunities you had. Without constantly bringing people from behind us, we won't continue to grow."

Fujitani is careful to acknowledge that it was franchisee extraordinaire Pete Harman whose values were enacted by all those who helped him along the way. "Pete has a magic touch that I don't think anyone will ever have again. He puts confidence in you that you never realized you had. He'll just put his arm around you and say, 'I know you can do it.' You ask him, 'How are we going to do this, Pete?' And he'll say, 'I know you'll find a way.' And by God, somehow we get it done."

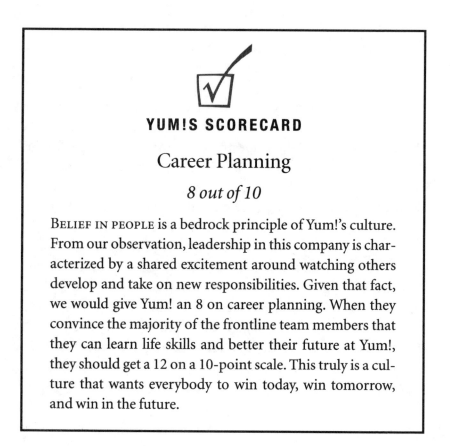

YUM!S SCORECARD

Career Planning

8 out of 10

BELIEF IN PEOPLE is a bedrock principle of Yum!'s culture. From our observation, leadership in this company is characterized by a shared excitement around watching others develop and take on new responsibilities. Given that fact, we would give Yum! an 8 on career planning. When they convince the majority of the frontline team members that they can learn life skills and better their future at Yum!, they should get a 12 on a 10-point scale. This truly is a culture that wants everybody to win today, win tomorrow, and win in the future.

TREAT YOUR
PEOPLE THE RIGHT WAY

SUMMARY STATEMENTS

If you treat your people the right way, they will treat your customers the right way so that your cash register goes ca-ching. How do you make that happen?

■ You have to integrate four human systems: recruiting and hiring, training and development, performance management, and career planning.

■ With effective recruiting and hiring, you get the right people on the team.

■ Effective training gets people the right start and helps them grow.

■ Performance management done the right way gets the people the right help when they need it so they can accomplish their goals and the organization can win.

- Without the right systems and processes, you can't do performance management the right way.

- Recognition on a day-to-day basis and celebrations of performance over time keep people inspired and focused on what's important.

- To keep people going, you have to have them growing. Career planning is an ongoing process.

- People are not your organization's most important resource; they *are* your organization.

CHAPTER 6

STEP FOUR
Have the Right Kind of Leadership

THE FOURTH AND FINAL STEP in building a customer-focused company the right way is developing the right kind of leadership. To pull off all the things I've been talking about requires a special kind of leader.

As I mentioned earlier, when I use the term *leader* I'm not just talking about the top dogs—CEOs, presidents, and directors. I'm talking about anyone who is in a position to influence others, for better or worse. While it is up to top leadership to set an organization's vision and direction, the day-to-day leadership falls to the hearts, heads, and hands of people at all levels.

BLANCHARD'S DREAM

To ME, the right kind of leader is a servant leader. Yet when people hear the phrase *servant leader,* often they are confused. They immediately conjure up thoughts of the inmates running the prison or trying to please everyone. Others think servant leadership is only for church leaders. The problem is that they don't understand leadership. They think you can't lead and serve at the same time. Yet you can if you understand—as I have emphasized a number of times—that there are two parts of leader-

149

ship: vision and implementation. When your vision is clear, you invert the pyramid and shift to a service frame of mind for implementation. Then you realize you are serving the vision and the people who are the foundation of your organization.

Just so you don't think that servant leadership can happen only in a church, let me give you a government example. I don't know about you, but I've had some real challenges in dealing with my state's Department of Motor Vehicles. They have such a multitude of people to take care of—basically, everybody with a driver's license—that it's no surprise they sometimes treat me like a number instead of a person. In most states, after passing the initial tests, you can avoid the DMV for a number of years if you fill out the proper form and mail it in. You're only required to show up in person at the DMV every ten years or so.

I avoided the DMV like the plague. But a few years ago, I lost my driver's license about three weeks before I was going on a trip to Europe. I knew I had to go to the DMV and get a new license to back up my passport on my trip. So I said to my executive assistant, "Dana, would you put three hours on my calendar next week sometime so I can go to the DMV?" That's about how long it takes them to beat you up. You wait for a long time and then they tell you you're in the wrong line, you've filled out the wrong form, or you've done something that means you have to start all over.

I headed over to the DMV with low expectations. Remember, I hadn't been there in years. I knew immediately something had changed when I walked in the front door, because a woman charged me and said, "Welcome to the Department of Motor Vehicles! Do you speak English or Spanish?"

I said, "English."

She said, "Right over there." The guy behind the counter

smiled and said, "Welcome to the Department of Motor Vehicles! How may I help you?" It took me nine minutes to renew my license, including getting my picture taken. I said to the woman who took my picture, "What are you all smoking here? I mean, this isn't the Department of Motor Vehicles that I used to know and love."

And she said, "Haven't you met the new director?"

I said, "No."

So she pointed to a desk behind all the counters, right out in the open. Clearly the director had no privacy. His office was in the middle of everything. I went over, introduced myself, and said, "What's your job as the director of the Department of Motor Vehicles?"

What he said is the best definition of management I've ever heard:

My job is to reorganize the department on a moment-to-moment basis depending on citizen (customer) need.

Isn't that a wonderful definition of a manager?

What did this director do? He cross-trained his people in everybody else's job. Everyone could handle the front desk; everyone could take the pictures. You name it, everyone could do it! Even the people in the back of the house that normally weren't out in front of the citizens could do everyone's job. Why? Because if suddenly there was a flood of citizens, why have people in the back doing bookkeeping, accounting, or

secretarial work, when there were customers who needed help? So he'd bring them out when they were needed.

You know what else my DMV director friend did? He insisted that nobody could go to lunch between 11:30 and 2:00. Why? Because that's when the customers show up. I was telling this story at a seminar one time and a woman came up to me on the break and said, "Where is your Department of Motor Vehicles? I can't believe what you've been telling us." She continued, "I was waiting in line for about forty-five minutes at our DMV and I was just about to get to the front of the line when the woman announced, 'It's break time.' And we had to stand around for fifteen minutes while they all went and got coffee and stretched their legs."

That didn't happen at my "new" Department of Motor Vehicles, where the director had created a motivating environment. Those team members were really committed. Even people I recognized from past visits who had joined in on the fun of abusing the customers were now excited about serving. Everyone can make a difference in the lives of your people. It's your choice whether you want to make a positive difference or a negative difference.

You can see somebody at one point who is so excited about work. Then you see that person three months later and they're depressed—their thoughts are in the toilet. In 90 percent of these cases the only thing that has changed is that they've gotten a new boss. Someone who jerks them around, doesn't listen to them, doesn't involve them in decision making, and treats them as if they really are *subordinate*. The same goes the other way. People can be unhappy in a job situation and suddenly a new leader comes in and their eyes brighten, their energy increases, and they are really ready to perform well and make a difference.

When you make a positive difference, people act like they own the place and they bring their brains to work. Their managers not only like that, but they encourage that kind of initiative. Another example from the "new" DMV punctuates this point.

LET YOUR PEOPLE BRING THEIR BRAINS TO WORK

Just about the time I had my inspiring experience with the DMV, Dana, my executive assistant, decided she was going to get a big motor scooter and bop around southern California. When she got this beauty somebody said to her, "You've got to get a license." She had never thought about needing a license for a motor scooter. So she went to the DMV to do the right thing. The woman behind the front counter went into the computer and found her name and driving record. It turns out that Dana had a perfect driving record. She never had a traffic violation.

"Dana," the woman said to her, "I noticed that in three months you're going to have to retake your written driving test. Why don't you take both tests today?"

Taken off guard, Dana said, "Tests? I didn't know I was supposed to take a test." And she started to panic.

This woman was beautiful. She reached over the counter, patted Dana's hand, and said, "Oh, Dana, don't worry. With your driving record, I'm sure you can pass these tests. And besides, if you don't you can always come back."

Dana took the tests. She went back to this woman, who scored her tests. Dana fell one correct answer short of passing each test, so officially she failed both tests. But in a kindly way the woman said, "Oh, Dana. You are so close to passing. Let me try something. Let me re-ask you one question on each test to see if you can get it right so I can pass you." Now that was a wonderful offer. But let me tell you one other thing. There were only two answers for each question. So the woman said, "Dana, you chose B. What do you think would be the right answer?"

When Dana said, "A!" this wonderful woman said, "You're right! You pass!"

I was telling this story one time at a seminar and this real bureaucrat comes racing up to the platform during the break. You know the type. Someone with real tight underwear on. He started yelling at me, "Why are you telling this story? That woman broke the law! Your assistant failed both of those tests!"

So I went back to see my DMV director friend. I told him about this bureaucrat and he said, "Ken, let me tell you one other thing. When it comes to decision-making, I want my people to use their brains more than rules, regulations, or laws. My person decided that it was silly to make someone like your assistant Dana, with her perfect driving record, come back to retake a test that she had only fallen one correct answer short of passing. I guarantee you, if she had missed four or five questions, my person wouldn't have given her the same deal. And to show you how important I think this is, *I would back that person's decision with my job.*"

Would any of you like to work for this kind of leader? You'd better believe everyone would. Why? Because he was a servant leader. In Rick Warren's wonderful book, *The Purpose Driven Life,* the first sentence is: "It's not about you." Just like our DMV director, servant leaders realize that. Leadership is not about them. It's about what and who they are serving. What's the vision, and who's the customer? Everyone has a customer.

Some people may only have external customers, while others—like personnel departments—only serve internal customers. Some departments, such as accounting, serve external and internal customers. Everyone has customers. Who's the customer for a manager? The people who report to that manager. Once the vision and direction are set, managers work for their people.

When I talk about servant leadership and ask people whether they are servant leaders or self-serving leaders, no one will admit to being a self-serving leader. And yet we observe self-serving leadership all the time. What is the difference?

DRIVEN VERSUS CALLED LEADERS

Gordon McDonald, in his book *Ordering Your Private World*, has an interesting distinction that can help us understand the difference between servant leaders and self-serving leaders. McDonald contends there are two kinds of people: driven people and called people. Driven people think they own everything. They own their relationships, they own their possessions, and they own their positions. Driven people are self-serving. Most of their time is spent protecting what they own. They run bureaucracies and believe the sheep are there for the benefit of the shepherd. They want to make sure that all the money, recognition, and power move up the hierarchy and away from the frontline people and the customers. They're great at creating duck ponds.

Called people are very different. They think everything is on loan—their relationships, possessions, and position. Do you know your relationships are on loan? One of the tough things about 9/11 was that some loans got called early. If you knew you might not see someone important in your life tomorrow, how would you treat that person? My wife, Margie, always says, "Keep your I-love-you's up to date."

Called people understand that possessions are only temporary. In tough economic times, a lot of people get uptight about losing their toys. They think "he who dies with the most toys wins." The reality is, "he who dies with the most toys dies." It's great to have nice things when things are going well, but you might have to give up some of them in hard times. Possessions are on loan.

Called leaders also understand that their positions are on loan from all the stakeholders in the organization, particularly the people who report to them. Since called leaders don't own anything, they figure their role in life is to shepherd everybody and everything that comes their way.

Self-serving leaders give themselves away in two ways: First, in how they receive feedback. Have you ever tried to give feedback to someone up the hierarchy and that person killed the messenger? If that has ever occurred, you were dealing with a self-serving leader. They hate feedback. Why? Because if you give them any negative feedback they think you don't want them to lead anymore. And that's their worst nightmare, because they *are* their position. The second giveaway for self-serving leaders is their unwillingness to develop other leaders around them. They fear the potential competition for their leadership position.

Called leaders have servant hearts and love feedback. They know the only reason they are leading is to serve, and if anybody has any suggestions how they can serve better, they want to hear. Their first response to feedback usually is, "Thank you.

That's really helpful. Could you tell me more? Is there anybody else I should talk to?"

Called leaders also are willing to develop others. Since they see their role in life is to serve, not to be served, they want to bring out the best in others. If a good leader rises up, servant leaders are willing to partner with that person, and even step aside and take a different role if necessary. They thrive on the development of others.

THE PLIGHT OF THE EGO

What keeps people from becoming servant leaders? It's the human ego. To me, ego stands for Edging God Out and putting yourself in the center. That's when we start to get a distorted image of our own importance and see ourselves as the center of the universe.

There are two ways our egos get in the way. One is *false pride,* when you start thinking more of yourself than you should. That's when you start pushing and shoving for credit and thinking leadership is about you rather than those who are led. You spend much of your time promoting yourself. The other way your ego trips you up is *self-doubt* or *fear*—thinking less of yourself than you should. Now you are consumed with your own shortcomings and are hard on yourself. You spend a great deal of time protecting yourself. With both false pride and self-doubt you have a hard time believing you are loved. Now you think your self-worth is a function of your performance plus the opinions of others. Since your performance will vary day-to-day and people are often fickle, with that belief your self-worth is up for grabs every day.

It's easy to understand that self-doubt comes from lack of

self-esteem because people afflicted with it on a daily basis act as if they are worth less than others. It is less obvious when people have false pride, because they behave as if they are worth more than others. People with false pride, who act as if they are the only ones who count, are really trying to make up for their own lack of self-esteem. They overcompensate for their "not okay" feelings by trying to control everything and everybody around them. In the process, they make themselves unlovable to those around them.

It's interesting for me to see how false pride and self-doubt play out in managers. When managers are addicted to either ego affliction, it erodes their effectiveness. Managers dominated by false pride are often called controllers. Even when they don't know what they are doing, they have a high need for power and control. Even when it's clear to everyone that they are wrong, they keep on insisting they are right. These folks aren't much for supporting their people, either. If everyone is upbeat and confident, the controller throws out the wet blanket. They support their bosses over their people because they want to climb the hierarchy and be part of the bosses' crowd.

At the other end of the spectrum are the do-nothing bosses. They are described as "never around, always avoiding conflict, and not very helpful." They often leave people alone even when those people are insecure and don't know what they are doing. Do-nothing bosses don't seem to believe in themselves or trust in their own judgment. They value others' thoughts more than their own—especially the thoughts of those they report to. As a result, they rarely speak out and support their own people. Under pressure they seem to defer to whomever has the most power.

If any of this sounds a bit too close for comfort, don't be

alarmed. Most of us have traces of both false pride and self-doubt because the issue is really ego. We are stuck, all alone, focusing only on ourselves. The good news is that there is an antidote for both.

EGO ANTIDOTE

The antidote for false pride is humility. True leadership—the essence of what people long for and want desperately to follow—implies a certain humble sincerity that is not only appropriate but which brings the best response from people.

Jim Collins supports this truth in *From Good to Great*. He found two characteristics that describe great leaders: *will* and *humility*. Will is the determination to follow through on a vision/mission/goal. Humility is the capacity to realize that leadership is not about the leader, it's about the people and what they need.

According to Collins, when things are going well for typical self-serving leaders, they look in the mirror, beat their chests, and tell themselves how good they are. When things go wrong, they look out the window and blame everyone else. On the other hand, when things go well for great leaders, they look out the window and give everybody else the credit. When things go wrong, these servant leaders look in the mirror and ask questions like, "What could I have done differently that would have allowed these people to be as great as they could be?" That requires real humility.

One of the keys, therefore, to becoming a servant leader is humility. Let me give you two definitions of humility. The first one appeared in Norman Vincent Peale's and my book, *The Power of Ethical Management:*

**People with humility don't think
less of themselves, they just think
about themselves less.**

So people who are humble have solid self-esteem.

The second definition of humility comes from a wise old Texan, Fred Smith, author of *You and Your Network:*

**People with humility don't deny their power,
but they recognize that it passes through
them, not from them.**

I love that concept of power passing through you, not from you. Too many people think that who they are is their position and the power it gives them. I learned that was not true from my father when I was a youngster. After being elected the president of the seventh grade, I walked into the house, proud as punch. My naval officer father said, "Congratulations, Ken. It's great to be president of the class. But now that you're president, don't ever use your position. Great leaders are people who others follow because they respect them and like them, not because they have power."

Where does your power come from? It's not from your position.

How many of you would like to make the world a better place for having been here? Okay, everyone would. Now let me ask: How many of you have a plan for how you're going to do that? I find very few people who have a plan. And yet you all can make the world a better place by the moment-to-moment decisions you make as you interact with the people you come in contact with at work, at home, or in the community.

Suppose you leave the house in the morning and someone yells at you. You have a choice point: You can yell back, or you can go and give that person a hug and wish him or her a good day. Someone cuts you off on the way to work. You have a choice point. Are you going to chase that person down and give them an obscene gesture, or are you going to send a prayer toward his or her car? We have choices all the time. Humility tames your judgmental nature and motivates you to reach out your hand to support and encourage others.

What's the antidote for fear? It's God confidence. How many of you have kids? How many of you love your kids? For how many of you does the love of your kids completely depend on their success? If they're successful you love them; if they're not, you won't? Few, if any, would agree. We all love our kids unconditionally, right? What if you accepted that unconditional love for yourself? You know God didn't make any junk? Did you know that you can't control enough, sell enough, make enough money, or have a big enough position to get any more love? You have all the love you need. All you have to do is open yourself up to it.

Too many leaders today think their success depends on how much wealth they have accumulated, the amount of recognition they have received, and the power and status they have. Let me say there is nothing inherently wrong with any of those things, as long as you don't identify who you are as those things. As an alternative I'd like you to focus on the opposite of each of those as you move from success to significance. What's the opposite of the accumulation of wealth? It's generosity of time, talent, treasure, and touch (reaching out to support others). What's the opposite of recognition? It's service. What's the opposite of power and status? It's loving relationships.

I've found over the years that when we focus only on success, we will never reach significance. That's the problem with self-serving leaders—they never get out of their own way. On the other hand, by focusing on significance—generosity, service, and loving relationships—you'll be amazed at how much success will come your way. Take Mother Teresa as an example. She could have cared less about accumulation of wealth, recognition, and status. Her whole life was focused on significance. And yet what happened? Success came her way. Her ministry received tremendous financial backing, she was recognized all over the world and given the highest status wherever she went. She was the ultimate servant leader. If you focus on significance first, your emphasis will be on people. Through that emphasis, success *and* results will follow.

HAVE THE RIGHT KIND
OF LEADERSHIP

SUMMARY STATEMENTS

- There are two aspects of leadership: vision/direction and implementation.

- While top leadership sets the vision and direction, anyone who is in a position to influence others can be a leader.

- There are two kinds of leaders. *Driven* leaders are self-serving; *called* or *servant leaders* serve others.

- Servant leaders take responsibility for developing a compelling vision; then invert the pyramid and move to the bottom as cheerleaders, supporters, and encouragers.

- Servant leaders learn to let go of false pride and self-doubt.

- The antidote for false pride is humility.

- The antidote for self-doubt is confidence resulting from the realization that you are unconditionally loved.

- Leadership isn't all about you; it's about serving the vision and the people who will make it come alive.

YUM!'S REALITY: LEADERSHIP

HAS THE LEADERSHIP AT YUM! been able to move the emphasis from success to significance? I think so. Their *both/and* philosophy about people and results suggests that they have. The company does not tolerate the traditional focus on results first with people considered a resource to be exploited. People with traditional business values who join them either change or leave. The story of Andy Pearson is a good illustration of someone who shifted his emphasis. Here was a leader whose first priority was the demand for top performance. But after working with David and the Yum! leadership, he found that a demand for top performance—far from being softened or undermined by a concern for people—can be immeasurably enhanced by it.

Twenty-three years ago, when he was president of PepsiCo, Andy Pearson was named by *Fortune* magazine as one of the ten toughest bosses in America. During the nearly fifteen years he ran PepsiCo, Pearson used his take-no-prisoners style to push revenues from $1 billion to $8 billion. His direct reports described Andy as brutally frank. He used intimidation to reach his numbers-driven goals, consistently firing 10 to 20 percent of his workforce.

When Tricon was formed, David Novak was excited about Andy joining the team as Yum!'s founding chairman and CEO, because Andy had tremendous knowledge of Wall Street and his achievements as a general manager and results-oriented financial manager were nothing short of brilliant. David held the reins as the keeper of the culture and the synergy that developed between David and Andy went way beyond one plus one equaling two. It didn't take Andy long to notice that David's focus on people and recognition inspired exceptional performance.

Andy loved the philosophy of everybody being a leader. During his tenure at PepsiCo he had focused on only the top one hundred leaders. At Yum! he realized that focusing on everybody in the organization created a company where everybody knew they could make a difference—and exceptional results followed.

So, Andy began changing his ways. He let go of his need to be the smartest guy in the room and broke the habit of dominating others. He started to listen to his team. Most importantly, he started to *serve* them. Andy role-modeled coaching and support. He went from dealing with only a small team of direct reports to interacting with people at all levels of the organization. Under the leadership of Pearson and Novak, Tricon increased its store-level margins and cut its debt in half. Andy Pearson didn't stop demanding results; he just started getting them by putting people first. He continues to believe that it's the job of a leader to get results, but leaders must "do it in a way that makes the organization a great place to work, instead of just taking orders and hitting this month's numbers."

What is the right kind of leadership? "Ultimately," Pearson says, "it's all about having genuine concern for the other person." He pauses. "There's a big difference between being tough and being tough-minded. It has to do with humility."

HUMILITY ROCKS

Lots of people think leadership is about the leader. It's not. Leadership is really about those who are led. As I said, true leadership—the essence of what people long for and want desperately to follow—implies a certain humble sincerity that is not only appropriate but which brings the best response from people. Leader after leader we talked to at Yum! realized that if you go in acting like you've got it all together—"I know all about this and you don't, let me tell you what to do"—people will shut down. You'll never get to see their best. On the other hand, they've learned if you share your vulnerability, if you give them the feeling that says, "You guys are the experts, I'm here to learn from you" (like David did with the KFC franchisees), then people will show up. That requires real humility.

There's the story about a minister who visits a parishioner's farm, one that used to be poorly kept. He is surprised to find it cleared, plowed, and resplendent with crops. The minister says to the farmer, "God's really done a great job here!" The farmer responds, "Yes, and you should have seen it when God had it by Himself!"

"I love that story," says Novak. "It shows how free will works. I've had incredible opportunities, but I've also taken advantage of what I've had. As a leader, I make my best decisions when I'm at the upper end of the mood state, because that's gratitude. My worst moments are when I get in power drive and let my ego rule. I work on trying to get into that upper state, because that's when you take the high ground and you're humble, and you can really be an effective leader."

David is a great admirer of Jim Collins, the author of *From Good to Great*. Not only did he get the company's leadership to see the power of the *both/and* philosophy, but he also got them to understand the importance of humility for effective leadership. When he talks about humility Collins writes, "The good-to-great leaders never wanted to become larger-then-life heroes. They never aspired to be put on a pedestal or become unreachable icons. They're seemingly *ordinary people quietly producing extraordinary results*." (Italics ours.)

From corporate executives to frontline team members, the leaders we met at Yum! were not pushing and shoving for power or status. They are good folks who have a genuine belief in people. Leadership at this company is about adding value and helping people get results by engaging and supporting others. It's called casting the shadow of leadership. The head coach sets the example and it cascades up and down the organization.

HAVING THEM DO IT

The power of self-discovery is fundamental to the Belief in People principle we found operating at all levels of Yum! The company's respect for team member intelligence and capability underscores this core belief. It's a given that executives do not have the lock on the corporate IQ.

Novak says, "Most executives stand up in their coats and ties and give slide presentations, saying things like, 'This is the situation, you've got problems with cleanliness in your restaurants. Your score is 42 percent,' or whatever. When you do it that way, there's no change. Self-discovery is the way to make change work."

The Yum! approach is to have people plot out the various pieces of their business graphically so they can see the big picture and come to their own conclusions. By using learning maps, people see the same facts that the leadership sees, and draw their own conclusions. Yum! believes that if their people see the same data the management sees, they'll draw the same (or better) conclusions. At that point there's no need to sell them on the information. They own it because they discovered it. Sam Walton said, "The more you know, the more you care."

One of David Novak's stories about his days as a PepsiCo executive reminds us of the words of the ancient philosopher:

Of the true leader the people will say, "We did it ourselves."

—Lao Tzu

The events of this story took place in an older PepsiCo plant in a tough part of town that insiders called Baltimore Fort Apache. The union was tough and there was racial tension in the plant. A blown-out neon Pepsi logo over the building signaled the state of things. "I went in there and I had a round table with the bottling plant guys," says Novak. "There were ten people in the room, and when I asked what's going on they started complaining. 'It takes us two and a half hours to get our trucks out. I can't get a forklift for my fountain truck. All the bottling can guys get better equipment than I get,' and so on. Everybody's whining. I listened to all this stuff, and finally one guy looks up at me and says, 'So what are you going to do?'

"I said, 'I'm not going to do anything. The only thing I'm going to do is to come back and see what *you've* done. I'll be back in six months, and I want to hear all about how you guys fixed all this stuff you've been talking about. I'll get Rod Gordon, the market unit manager, to work with you, and you guys are going to fix this.'

"One of the best days in my career was six months later when I came back. I asked for the exact same people in the room, and they showed me what they had done. They showed me how they cut the truck loading times down significantly, and all the rest. It was just a real gratifying thing. These guys had been so negative and boy, when I came back their chests were popping out, and it was a great thing. They did it! They fixed it, and that was it."

Larry Bossidy, former Honeywell CEO and author of *Execution: The Discipline of Getting Things Done,* says it best: "You take the joy of the doing and deciding away, you take the joy of the job away."

CASCADING: HOW SERVANT LEADERS COMMUNICATE THROUGH TEACHING

When Yum! leaders want to communicate something important to the whole organization, they don't rely solely on memos or the communication department or any of the usual organizational communication vehicles. They design a teaching package that contains all they need to teach their people: training design, videos, and other materials. Senior management is taught the concepts and skills first.

It is then the leader's responsibility to teach their people. Their people are then charged with cascading the concept or skill on through the organization. David Novak describes how cascading works:

"We had this great meeting in Blackberry, Tennessee, and the team said, 'Well, what are we going to do with this?' Half the people said we have to take it onto the next level. The other half said, 'Our people won't be in Blackberry, and they won't have the same feeling, so it won't work.' We decided we were going to take it to the next level. Everybody loved it—and then guess what? Half the people said we should take it to the next level, and half of them said we shouldn't!

"We ended up cascading it throughout the organization right on to three thousand RGMs. It worked. Our leaders facilitated the process; we didn't have external people do it. We cascaded the ideas through the organization with our own leaders. Now we do the same thing with any major initiative that we want to communicate throughout the organization. After leaders teach, they step aside and let their people take over."

The cascading technique works particularly well overseas. "We launched four core cascades about being a Customer Maniac," reported Gregg Dedrick, "going down to all our employees around the world, company, or franchise. This is how we drive Customer Mania in the restaurants. Not only are we getting very high participation rates from franchisees, but people overseas tend to gravitate toward these things faster than the domestic people. They often don't have as many resources so if something looks good they latch onto it and do it. They have much more openness in being able to say, 'Let's take this and run with it.' "

KEEPING THE TEAM TOGETHER

When Taco Bell chief marketing officer Greg Creed talks about effective leadership, he says he's come to believe that the first requirement is courage to do the right thing. "When sales are down," Creed says, "Wall Street hollers. The temptation is to go for short-term glory or the large bonus check. The old way," he says, "was *first deliver the results*. The new way is, *do the right thing*."

The vowels AI/AE are used to designate a framework for decision making at Taco Bell's marketing department. Creed translates: "They stand for *Always Innovating, Always Elevating*. When we come up with an idea we first ask, '*Is it innovative?*' If it is, fine, but it's got to be *elevating,* too."

One of the great annoyances for people in business is that many of the decisions their bosses make are less about what matters and more about their careers. A framework like *I-and-E* serves to depersonalize the issue. It's an example of a clearly articulated system that provides better answers, and it marshals the best that is in the people who are involved.

Greg Creed shared with us the effect this has had on his department at Taco Bell and, ultimately, on the breakthrough sales success of the brand. "People love clarity. Clarity leads to commitment and gives them confidence. With our *I-and-E* decision filter, you can leave it up to people to make the right decision more often. It's been amazing to me to see how the clarifying and cascading of our brand's journey has made our 80-person marketing team come alive.

"When I came in here you'd hear comments like, 'Oh, he isn't committed,' or 'She's hard to work with.' But those people who were griping have turned around, and they're stars now. Looking at the success we've had financially the past three years shows that if you put doing the right thing first, the results will follow."

DOING IT YOUR WAY

In designing an organization that gets the best from its people, the company uses alternately loose and tight systems. While there are rigorous requirements where values are concerned, we found that when it came to day-to-day problem solving, people were enjoying a sense that they could do it their own way. "One of the vibrancies of our culture," Emil Brolick says, "is people being individuals. The commitment we share brings out, rather than suppresses, the character and talents of each individual. Far from trying to destroy individualism, everybody's trying to support it even more. It's a win-win when people feel great about themselves. It allows them to be individuals and achieve their own individual objectives in the context of a large organization that also has an objective. It becomes the enabler to exceptional performance."

Doing it your way sponsors a sense of pride. The person feels, I can make it better. I can do it faster, neater, more pleasingly. I can delight someone with the way I do it. If I am dealing directly with a customer, I have an opportunity, through my creativity, my cheerfulness, and my willingness to go the extra mile, to make that person's day. My opportunities to serve others—peers, teammates, managers, customers—opens the way for me to improve the task, to put my special mark on it, to do it flawlessly.

FROM ME TO WE

Helping people to soar like eagles (instead of quack like ducks) means focusing on the needs of other persons and sending a clear message that you care for them. David Novak uses another heartwarming phrase for this. He calls it "moving from me to we."

One of the ways "me to we" manifests itself at Yum! is "telling on yourself." People tell on themselves all the time, and they tell on each other. Dave Deno tells on himself with great regularity. Jerry Buss tells on Aylwin Lewis. In a business-as-usual organization, people say, "I didn't do it" when mistakes are made, and take credit when the good stuff comes around. In a very refreshing way, this company reverses that. When there's credit to be taken, you hear, "I didn't do it"—somebody else did it, my team, somebody at another brand. The only time they take credit is when they screw up. And even then they tell how someone else bailed them out.

Telling on yourself is one of the ways the Customer Mania culture is spread and reinforced. It makes leaders vulnerable and available to their people. It opens up communication. It generates respect. Usually we think, "If I admit failure, I'll lose respect." But it actually works just the opposite.

LISTEN AND LEARN

Paul Coffman is a regional coach for Pizza Hut in Dallas. He oversees eight area coaches, who in turn coach an average of ten RGMs. Coffman says:

"As I coach my team, if I come across an individual who's having a tough time feeling comfortable and recognizing people, I see it as an opportunity to make that person feel better about himself. Once he feels good about himself, he has no problem allowing others to feel good about themselves. Especially when we're working with the most challenging opportunities, we have to pay attention to keeping the person we're coaching feeling good about him or herself.

"If I'm going to ask somebody a question, I'd better have my slate clean to listen as long as it takes for them to get their point across. My own agenda, if I've got one at all, is secondary. After all, they know the business far better than I do, so I just listen and learn."

We asked Coffman about his use of the term *opportunities*. "You want to get people looking at what they're doing right," he says. "Our business is fast paced. Successes are short lived. Once you feel good about one thing, you feel like you're in a snake pit about something else. Every day our people meet a lot of tough or perplexing situations. You could call them problems or deficiencies, but those words don't fit the language of self-confidence. An *opportunity* is something that we can all use to get better. Why not concentrate on using ideas that keep you feeling the best you can? I always say, look at what you're doing right."

LEADER-LED CULTURE

As I've said before, a lot of people don't think the words *servant* and *leader* can go together. Yum! has proved that they do. They have been impeccable in setting their vision and then doing everything they can to invert the pyramid and adopt a service mindset to implement the vision. At the same time, they don't abdicate their leadership role of setting and communicating the vision. Leaders are essential in the vision area. As Irfan Mustafa, who runs the Middle East business, puts it:

"Culture has to be leader led. This is something that can't be delegated. It has to be initiated by our very most senior leaders. Secondly, it has to be cascaded. You can't skip a level when you're driving what's really important. It's got to be leader led and the leaders have to cascade the culture all the way to the person that touches our customers."

"It's a never-ending journey," says Pizza Hut president Peter Hearl. "You can't ever stop or let up on it. The job's never done. You've got to continually look for ways and means to take it to the next level because there are a lot of people who are either looking for it not to work or leaders who don't place as much emphasis or focus on the culture.

"There are a lot of people who say it can't be done, or don't want it to be done. But you've got to believe. Leaders who believe in what they're doing stay focused. They stay the course and go the distance."

YUM!'S SCORECARD

Leadership

10 out of 10

WHEN IT COMES to leadership, Yum! gets a 10. They have created a compelling vision and then inverted the pyramid to help everyone make it come alive. Wherever we went in the organization, in every brand we found leaders who are willing to serve. They all seem to be passionate about the vision to put a Yum! on faces worldwide. They are committed to the *How We Work Together* principles and to building an organization the right way. We didn't find anyone on a power trip, determined to keep the traditional hierarchal pyramid right side up during implementation of the vision. Yum!'s leaders believe in people, realizing and appreciating that Customer Mania is the goal. And yet their emphasis is not just on people, but also on results. They want to be a high-performing organization in every way. We found it pretty amazing how well the leadership approach at the top has been cascaded throughout the organization.

PART III

Next Steps

CHAPTER 7

The High Hurdle

Cracking the Code on Customer Mania

HYRUM SMITH, founder of Franklin-Quest and author of *What Matters Most*, once shared with me an insight about getting things done. He said:

Character is following through on a good decision after the excitement of making the decision has passed.

A lot of people love to make announcements. Yet it's commitments, not announcements, that really matter. Commitment has to do with making sure that what we intend to do or what we announce gets done. A lot of people are interested in building a customer-focused, high-performing organization, but always have an excuse why they can't do it. Committed people don't know about excuses—all they know about is results. They want to do what they say they're going to do. That's what we think David Novak and his people are: committed to proving that it's never too late to build a customer-focused company the right way. But as they are the first to admit, this is a journey, and they still have a way to go.

We believe Yum! has a world-class leadership group and systems in place to take it to greatness. However, the company has one major hurdle it must clear to fully actualize its vision: it must drive Customer Mania through the roofs into every one of its restaurants around the world. To crack the code on Customer Mania and put a Yum! on everyone's face, the company must master three key practices:

1. Developing passionate, engaged team members.

2. Acting as one system around the world.

3. Execute, execute, execute.

Next, we examine each of these practices, together with how well the company is doing on them.

PRACTICE NO. 1: DEVELOPING PASSIONATE, ENGAGED TEAM MEMBERS

WHILE THE LEADERSHIP OF YUM! has done an admirable job cascading their Customer Mania vision down through the coaching hierarchy, the rubber will meet the road when they have passionate and engaged team members on the frontline of every restaurant. After all, it's these team members who have the day-to-day interaction with the customers and will either be gung ho and put a Yum! on customers' faces, or act like uncommitted hired hands and be non-factors or—even worse—turn customers off.

When the latter occurs, not only is Customer Mania thwarted and growth of same store sales jeopardized, but turnover becomes an issue. You can't run consistently great restaurants and create Customer Mania with soaring turnover rates. If people are leaving, you obviously don't have passionate, engaged team members. And without passionate, engaged team members, this company will never put a Yum! on every customer's face.

Aylwin Lewis says, "We are too good not to be great. And we should be great; the customer should be noticing. A big driver of that is retention inside the restaurants. At 114 percent turnover we

are never going to create Customer Maniacs. So we have to cut
turnover. We have to keep our better people. We think that 50 percent is the target; we think we can get to 50 percent. But we need to
do things incredibly differently.

"Right now there's a disparity, a disconnect for team members,"
Aylwin continues. "We have a pretty good deal for RGMs and above.
You're an owner, your career is in your hands, you can grow. Com-
bining salary and bonus you can make $50,000 a year, and you have
stock options. Contrast this with what the team members feel. If
you're a team member, a lot still depends on the type of RGM you
have. Team members need to have the same sense of ownership as
leaders. What we struggle with is, 'If the values are the core, how do I
make it better for everybody?'

"Once people are welcomed aboard, how they are treated is the
key," Aylwin says. "Our surveys show that not many people leave because they get more money someplace else. They might if they could
find two dollars an hour more someplace else, but usually it's just
ten or fifteen cents more. Most of the time the reason for turnover
has to do with how they have been treated and what kind of manager is in place. It's that special person who recognizes you and sends
you birthday cards that makes the difference."

The founders of Yum! had a chance to build a great customer-
focused company, and they carefully considered what kind of company it should be. After previewing a broad spectrum of reasons why
certain companies had turned out to be great, David Novak and his
cofounders decided that their organization would be based on an
unwavering belief in people and that it would provide opportunities
for each of its constituents to be as good as he or she could be. In this
respect Yum! Brands echoes the dream of America. It continues to
demonstrate that the days are not over when anyone, starting with
nothing but willingness and persistence, can build a satisfying life
and career to be proud of. If the company can sell this dream to new
team members, their turnover might drop dramatically.

PRACTICE NO. 2: ACTING AS ONE SYSTEM
AROUND THE WORLD

THE SECOND KEY to achieving the company's goal is instituting one vision—Customer Mania—to people not only in the United States but in many different cultures. With 33,000 restaurants in the United States and more than 100 countries and territories around the world, Yum!'s challenge is obvious.

The first hurdle is geographic. Having a great base to grow from, the company is pushing to increase its presence internationally. The question is, to what degree will its rah-rah Customer Mania culture excite people outside United States borders? The franchisee system represents a second hurdle, presenting both human relations and technical challenges. To what degree will Yum!'s culture excite franchisees?

The company has made great strides toward achieving a unified system internationally. According to Pat Murtha, formerly chief people officer of Yum! Restaurants International and now head coach at Pizza Hut, the *How We Work Together* culture has become better embedded internationally than here in the United States:

"It's just taken hold," Pat says. "People have found something about it that is very attractive to them. In most of our markets the RGMs hold a very special role; in Malaysian cultures they are hallowed positions. The fact that most of those managers embraced and cascaded the *How We Work Together* principles is what's made such a big difference. They've owned the culture, it's been led and sponsored by them, and it's amazing how well it's been received."

David Novak tells a story about a recent trip to Singapore that reveals why he's gung ho about meeting the international challenge. "I was with my wife, Wendy, in Singapore for a franchisee meeting. After the meeting we walked into a KFC that was in the mall to meet some of the people. As we were walking out to go do a little shopping, an area coach—her name was Carol Tang—started yelling,

'Mr. Novak, Mr. Novak, Mr. Novak!' And she came over. I told her not to call me Mr. Novak, to call me David.

"She said, 'I want you to know how much I appreciate what's going on in our company. I've learned so much about myself.' And she pulled out her *I will* card. We do these *I will* cards in our training; after you go through the training, you declare, 'I will do this, do that' or whatever. She said, 'I've learned that I need to listen to my people better. I'm going to be a better coach.' And then she told me about the four things that she's working on.

"This is Singapore, and I'm from Louisville, Kentucky. I pull out my own *I will* card and I read it to her, telling her what I'm working on. Later, as Wendy and I walked on to go shopping, she said, 'Do you realize what's going on in this company? Here you have the chairman of the company and an area coach, and she can come up and have a conversation about how she is going to be a better leader and you get to share what you're doing.' After she said that, I thought to myself, It doesn't get any better than this!"

Despite predictions that recognition wouldn't work in Asia's more formal cultures, the *How We Work Together* principles have taken off there and everywhere around the globe. The recognition symbols—especially Novak's personal Walk-the-Talk Award, a huge set of teeth mounted on a pair of spindly legs—have been a hit in every country. In some cases, the awards become precious family treasures. On a trip to China, vice president of operations excellence Shirlie Kunimoto met a restaurant manager who had received an award. When Shirlie asked the RGM if she could see the award, the woman replied, "No, I can't show it to you."

"Why not?" asked Shirlie.

"Because," the woman said, "it's locked up in my father's safe at home."

Sam Su, president of the Greater China division, reports that this division is growing at more than three hundred restaurants a year. "It is true that in China—given years of authoritarian rule and a very rigid structure—people are more used to hierarchal managerial relationships," says Su. "But the young people want to build a future of their own and show they can be good leaders. Their aspirations on our team are even stronger, I think, than in other cultures." Does the Customer Mania culture play in China? Absolutely. In fact, on January 19, 2004, one thousand RGMs came together and created the world's largest Yum! cheer on The Great Wall to mark the one-thousandth KFC in China.

These successes internationally reflect the company's progress in creating a unified system. "The secret of our success is that the culture is standardized, very single-minded," says George Ting, a franchisee in Asia. "While we have some room to be innovative, as far as the franchise business—the operations systems, the marketing direction—we are one system."

Andrew Partridge, senior vice president, Yum! Restaurants International, sums it up. "Diversity within unity creates business advantage," he says.

There is strong evidence that the Yum! culture and the Partnership Pact have created tremendous synergy between franchisee and franchisor in the United States as well. For example, the company combined all the brands—company and franchisee stores together—to buy food supplies through what has become the largest food cooperative in the industry, securing enormous savings. "We have great power," says Chris Campbell, Yum! general counsel. "But that power never could have happened if the franchisees didn't feel comfortable coming together with us. We're the envy of the industry because this has led to tremendous cooperative relations among the brands and stores."

PRACTICE NO 3: EXECUTE, EXECUTE, EXECUTE

THE FINAL AND MOST IMPORTANT key for Yum! to achieve its goal of Customer Mania is to continue doing what they have been doing. As

David Novak puts it, "We know what our passion is. We've identified our formula for success. We've defined how we need to lead. And we've clearly articulated how we will win and how we work together. No one in our industry has more potential to reap the benefits of running great restaurants. But potential means you haven't done it yet. Execution is the biggest challenge we face. The difference between good and great lies in the daily intensity we bring to executing our own strategies."

Novak is always challenging, always raising the bar. And yet we didn't find anyone backing off. "We are too good not to be great" was a phrase we often heard around Yum! We feel they already have a great vision. They already have a structure for treating their customers and people right. They already have the initiatives, systems, processes, and tools to make the company great. The company must put these practices to use on a moment-to-moment basis to bring the dream of Customer Mania alive.

"We don't need to develop any new processes," says David Novak. "We know what to do to drive the business—we've done a lot of the tough sledding. What we need to do now is execute, execute, execute."

✳

Developing passionate, engaged team members, acting as one system around the world, and executing, executing, executing are the three practices the company must master before it can drive the Customer Mania culture through the roof of every restaurant—both company and franchisee—and make the vision of the global Yum! Dynasty a reality. From our vantage point, they've made a great start.

CHAPTER 8

It's Your Choice
The Yum! Door or the Dumb Door?

THERE ARE TWO WAYS to approach business: By going through the Yum! door or the dumb door. Before the do-over, Yum! was a huge, unwieldy, fractured organization—a mixed bag getting mixed results. They were going through the dumb door. Now people in the organization are aligned and on the road to someplace special because they have decided to go through the Yum! door. If they can do it, your organization can do it, too.

THE VISION OF THE YUM! DOOR

While this book is not about David Novak, no one would deny his effectiveness in articulating an inspiring company vision. He is at the heart of things; he's the Yum! Brands dream keeper. David articulates what life beyond the Yum! door could mean:

"When Yum! equals *You Understand Me,* people at all levels of our organization will be more passionate and proud. They won't want to work anywhere else. Then our customers will walk in and go, 'Wow! What happened to this place? This is so different from what it used to be. The people here actually *care* about us!' "

Going through the Yum! door means balancing concern for people with concern for results, and making sure that the first drives the second.

"It's very humbling for me," David said, "to go to meetings

186

around the world and see that in our own small way this company is helping to make the world a better place for so many families. Maybe it's only ten thousand families, maybe it's five thousand, but there's a noble cause to this work.

"This is a tough industry, tougher than I ever talk about or admit, because I'm always out there selling a dream. What keeps me up at night is the possibility of our not getting the results we need to carry this on. You're not considered a good coach unless your team scores runs. People believe in winners; winning gives you the credibility to continue. I tell people it's a lot more fun to do Yum! cheers when stock is 72 than when it's 23. They all laugh, but it's true. I think in the end the real measure of our success will be the extent to which our customers are raving about us. When that happens, our profits will be through the roof and we will be winning. A continued rising stock price will be a big part of it, because that's part of winning."

Many readers will think that building a customer-focused company along the lines of Yum!'s would be difficult and fraught with effort. That's because they're still thinking of leadership as pushing and efforting—*trying to get people to do things.* When results drive people, rather than the other way around, you will get that strain. Everything will be an effort. But putting results first is backward. Organizations and leaders who emphasize results at the expense of people are simply not riding the horse in the direction it is going.

Once you turn that around, the efforting goes away. You're operating in a way that restores energy rather than depleting it. It's true that we found very hard-working people at Yum!, but they didn't strike us as being tired or acting beat-up. Instead, they were passionate about what they were doing. When you are doing what you love, you never work a day in your life. Companies like Yum! defy the laws of physics, creating a perpetual-motion machine where the work feeds the energy, which feeds the work, which feeds the energy.

As we studied this organization, we began to ask ourselves some interesting questions. *Are these people somehow special? Is David Novak a one-of-a-kind leader? Can other organizations really achieve this level of commitment?* The same questions are asked about so-called unbeatable teams in sports. Are they really more talented than other teams? Sometimes yes, but more often the answer is no. They only look more gifted, because they are playing full out. They're passionately at their peak. Nothing is wasted.

If you want to get passion from people, make them number one.

That's the secret, right there. When you take the steps to building a customer-focused company, you make people better than they are. Suddenly your team is more interested in the enterprise; more giving of their discretionary time, ideas, and effort. Suddenly they're more talented. It's your choice: the Yum! door or the dumb door.

THE DIFFERENCE BETWEEN THE YUM! DOOR AND THE DUMB DOOR

What's the difference between the Yum! door and the dumb door? It's how you approach the four steps necessary to building a customer-focused company the right way.

Step 1: Set Your Sights on the Right Target. If you go through the dumb door, there is only one target: making money. The bottom line is the bottom line. The customers and your people are not considered part of the target. They are a means to an end at best.

When you go through the Yum! door, the right target is the triple bottom line. You believe that profit is the applause you get for taking care of your customers and creating a motivating environment for your people. The aim is to be the Provider of Choice (create raving fans), the Employer of Choice (having people who are Customer Maniacs), and the Investment of Choice (your cash registers are going ca-ching). The both/and philosophy is critical here. The choice is not between people and results; the emphasis is on both.

Step 2: Treat Your Customers the Right Way. When you go through the dumb door, your customers are a bother. In fact, people start to think their business would be a good place to work if they didn't have customers. Their customers get the message fast: "You're in the way."

When you go through the Yum! door, all your energy is focused on your customers. You want to create a Customer Mania culture. You realize that satisfying customers is not enough—you want them to be raving fans. You are constantly gathering stories of ways your people have gone the extra mile to create customers who want to brag about you. Why? Because the customers write everyone's check. They are the reason for your existence.

Step 3: Treat Your People the Right Way. When you go through the dumb door, you think of your managers as superiors and their people as subordinates. You even talk about the head of the department and the "hired hands." People don't even get a head. When there are tough economic times, downsizing and getting rid of people is the immediate response. People are expendable. Performance on the bottom line is essential.

When you go through the Yum! door, you realize that without your people you are nothing. You know it takes excited and passionate people to create raving fans and a Customer Mania culture. You believe in the Golden Rule and know that you can't treat your people poorly and expect them to take care of your customers. Empowering your people and permitting them to act as owners is essential. At the end of the day, when your people leave your premises, so does your business.

Step 4: Have the Right Kind of Leadership. When you go through the dumb door, you find leaders for whom humility is a lost art. When things go well, they look in the mirror and pound themselves on the chest; when things go poorly, they look out the window to find others to blame. They are self-serving. They act as if the sheep are there for the benefit of the shepherd and all the money, recognition, power, and status moves up the hierarchy. Leadership is all about them.

When you move through the Yum! door, you realize that leadership is not about you. You know you are only as good as your people. While you play a major role in setting the vision and direction, your goal is to move as quickly as possible to the bottom of the hierarchy, where you can cheerlead, support, and serve. Rather than focusing on accumulation of wealth, recognition, power, and status, the leaders you find through the Yum! door are focused on generosity of their time, talent, thinking, treasure, and touch. They are more concerned about serving than recognition; more interested in loving relationships than power and status. They coach first and coach second. Everything they do is to help people win, because they know if their people win, their organization wins.

✳

You might say I've depicted two extremes. Maybe so, but which direction do you want to go? I say move through the Yum! door and start the journey to building a customer-focused company. Remember, it's never too late. If a complicated, massive organization like Yum! Brands can create a customer-focused company the right way, so can you. Be committed, not interested. Go for it!

ACKNOWLEDGMENTS

THIS BOOK WOULD never have happened were it not for the support and encouragement of the following people. Special thanks go to David Novak, Aylwin Lewis, Gregg Dedrick, Jonathan Blum, and all the top managers of Yum!, whose enthusiasm and cooperation were invaluable. We are also grateful to Jeff Lightburn for his early championing of the book and to Rick Fallon for helping to move it along.

Big thanks to Fred Hills, editor and author enthusiast of the Free Press at Simon & Schuster. Thanks also to our in-house editor, Martha Lawrence, for her enthusiasm, dedication, and talent during the preparation of the final manuscript, and to Richard Andrews, Humberto Medina, Dottie Hamilt, Anna Espino, and the bestseller marketing team at The Ken Blanchard Companies.

The Blanchard's Dream sections contain a good summary of Ken's thinking over the years about leadership, management, and the development of great organizations. Being a lifelong learner, he wants to acknowledge those authors, scholars, and practitioners who have impacted the concepts and theories he espouses. These include Jim Belasco, Richard Nelson Bolles, Larry Bossidy, Sheldon Bowles, Bob Buford, Don Carew, John Carlos, Jan Carlzon, Truett Cathy, Jim Collins, Steve Covey, Max DePree, Wayne Dyer, Susan Fowler, Robert Greenleaf, Gary Heil, Paul Hersey, Phil Hodges, Bill Hybels, Spencer Johnson, Herb Kelleher, Thad Lacinak, Bob Lorber, Gordon McDonald, Michael O'Connor, George Ordiorne, Eunice Parisi-Carew, Norman Vincent Peale, Alan Randolph, Bob Russell, Horst Schulze, Don Shula, Fred Smith, Hyrum Smith, Ralph Stayer, Jesse Stoner, Rick Tate, Chuck Tompkins, Noel Tichy, Art Turock,

Terry Waghorn, Sam Walton, Rick Warren, Drea Zigarmi, and Pat Zigarmi.

We are immensely grateful to the most important people in our lives: Ken to his life partner of more than forty years, Margie; Jim to his "writing house family," Ba and Tani; and Fred to Calla, his friend, partner, and wife. We are blessed to know and love them.

ABOUT THE AUTHORS

Ken Blanchard is the chief spiritual officer of The Ken Blanchard Companies, a worldwide human resource development company. He is the author of several bestselling books, including the blockbuster international bestseller *The One Minute Manager* and the giant business bestsellers *Raving Fans, Gung Ho!,* and *Whale Done!* His books have combined sales of more than fifteen million copies in more than twenty-five languages. He is also cofounder of the Center for Faithwalk Leadership, a nonprofit ministry dedicated to inspiring and equipping people to lead like Jesus. Few people have made a more positive and lasting impact on the day-to-day management of people and companies than Ken Blanchard. He and his wife, Margie, live in San Diego and work with their son Scott, daughter Debbie, and Debbie's husband, Humberto Medina.

Jim Ballard has enjoyed careers as an educator, author, corporate trainer, consultant, and seminar designer. His books *What's the Rush?* and *Mind Like Water* have helped people put their lives in perspective. He also coauthored, with Ken Blanchard, Thad Lacinak, and Chuck Tompkins, the bestselling book *Whale Done!: The Power of Positive Relationships.* He has worked closely with Ken Blanchard and his coauthors on a number of writing projects, including *Mission Possible,* with Terry Waghorn; *Everyone's a Coach,* with Don Shula; and *Managing by Values,* with Michael O'Connor. He lives in Amherst, Massachusetts, and is active as a hospice volunteer and Big Brother.

Fred Finch is the author of *Managing for Organizational Effectiveness: An Experiential Approach.* He is also a coauthor, with Ken Blanchard and Pat Stewart, of Situational Frontline Leadership, a popular Blanchard training program for frontline leaders. A co-founding consulting partner of The Ken Blanchard Companies, he has been a consultant and leadership educator at Harvard University, Merrill Lynch, IBM, Shell International, and many other high-profile organizations. He received his doctorate from the Graduate School of Business at the University of Washington and served as a professor of management and organizational behavior for fourteen years in the Graduate School of Management at the University of Massachusetts, Amherst.

SERVICES AVAILABLE

The Ken Blanchard Companies is committed to helping people and organizations lead at a higher level. With a mission to *unleash the power and potential of people and organizations for the greater good,* the company is a global leader in workplace learning, productivity, and leadership effectiveness. The Ken Blanchard Companies believes that people are the key to accomplishing strategic objectives. Its programs not only help people learn, but also ensure that they cross the bridge from learning to doing. The company offers seminars and provides in-depth consulting in the areas of teamwork, customer service, leadership, performance management, and organizational synergy. To learn more, visit the website at www.kenblanchard.com or browse the eStore at www.kenblanchard.com/estore

The Ken Blanchard Companies
125 State Place
Escondido, CA 92029
800-728-6000 or 760-489-5005
Fax: 760-489-8407

The Center for Faithwalk Leadership, of which Ken Blanchard is cofounder, is a nonprofit ministry dedicated to inspiring and equipping people to walk their faith in the marketplace. The ministry offers seminars, learning materials, and simulcast celebrations that are available through a satellite broadcasting system. To learn more, visit the website at www.leadlikejesus.com.

The Center for Faithwalk Leadership
1229 Augusta W. Parkway
Augusta, GA 30909
800-383-6890 or 706-863-8494
Fax: 760-489-1332